THE INCREDIBLY STRANGE
BOOK OF
HORRIBLE FACTS

THE INCREDIBLY STRANGE

BOOK OF

HORRIBLE FACTS

ARCTURUS

ARCTURUS

This edition published in 2014 by Arcturus Publishing Limited
26/27 Bickels Yard, 151–153 Bermondsey Street,
London SE1 3HA

ISBN: 978-1-78404-318-6
CH004304NT
Supplier 29, Date 0614, Print Run 3532

Written by Alex Woolf, Anne Rooney, Helen Otway and Marc Powell
Design and illustration by Dynamo and Steve Beaumont
Additional design by JMS Books

Printed in China

CONTENTS

Read on ... if you dare!

Welcome to this collection of the grossest, most yucky, and truly vomit-inducing facts to ever be gathered together in one place! You may have thought you had experienced disgusting things before. Maybe you had a nasty sickness bug, or you know someone who can burp really loudly, but nothing could have prepared you for these absolutely vile, off-the-scale horrible facts!

For instance, did you know that there is a jellyfish so poisonous to humans that it can cause a brain to bleed? Or that in some places in the world, people eat the brains of their dead relatives? Have you heard about the Russian ruler, Ivan the Terrible, who had a habit of brutally murdering members of his own family? And did you know that when a frog is sick, its entire stomach comes up and ends up hanging outside its mouth?

If the answer to any of these is "no" you need to read this book! Hold on tight as we journey through the most disgusting diseases and functions of the human body. Gasp in horror at the gruesome experiments and ghastly developments in the world of science. Shudder at our despicable ancestors and the dreadful conditions recorded throughout history. Be repulsed by the disgusting habits of animals and the horrific hunters of the animal kingdom, and finally, try to hold it together for a last dip into the most appalling collection of random horrible facts!

You have had fair warning of the contents of this book. Before you read any further, it is best to prepare yourself. You will need a bucket, some newspaper, and make sure you keep all of the lights on!

Ready to be horrified? Then read on...

Don't try this at home!

Even though some of these facts sound really cool, do NOT try them at home. No matter how fun it is to read about these things, the reality is quite nasty. The people in this book who have performed stunts or eaten yucky food on purpose have trained for a long time to be able to do this. Do not think that you would be able to eat hundreds of scorpions and be okay. Read the book, enjoy the facts, but leave the weird stuff to the experts.

Incredibly Strange Body Facts

When you sneeze, the air coming out of your nose and mouth travels at the same speed as a category 2 hurricane: 160 km (100 miles) an hour!

French doctor Frédéric Saldmann insists that people should burp, fart, and sweat freely to reduce the risk of cancer.

Your nose is busy making mucus all day long, but you swallow most of it – about one cupful. Gross!

Earwax tastes very bitter. If you must try it, make sure no one's looking...

British man Graham Butterfield has such a sensitive bottom that he tests beds for a living. He has insured his behind for £1 million, thats around US$1.6 million!

Your body makes a new skin every month – that means you'll get through about 1,000 skins in your lifetime!

In the last minute, at least 30,000 dead skin cells have fallen off your body. You lose about 50 million every day!

Some perfumes contain ambergris. Sounds nice? It's whale vomit!

In space, astronauts use specially formulated toothpaste – they can't spit it out, they have to swallow all the froth. Gross!

You sweat all day long, even when you don't feel it. As you read this, more than two million sweat glands around your body are working to keep it at the right temperature.

What you hear when you fart is the vibration of your sphincter muscles as air passes through them. The sort of sound you get depends on how fast the air is moving.

Poisons can give you great-looking skin! Botulinum toxin (Botox) is famous for its wrinkle-smoothing effects, but if you don't like needles, there is a cream that mimics snake venom and gives similar results.

Touch signals travel to the brain more quickly than pain signals. That's why you feel the bump from stubbing your toe before the agony sets in!

It takes six hours for a coating of plaque to form after cleaning your teeth. If you don't brush it off, it eventually becomes tartar: a rock-hard substance that your dentist has to scrape off.

A 127-kg (280-lb)-German man was saved by his rolls of fat when he was shot during a mugging – the bullet lodged itself in the fat and he was uninjured.

If you cut yourself, your body will produce one million extra cells an hour until it heals.

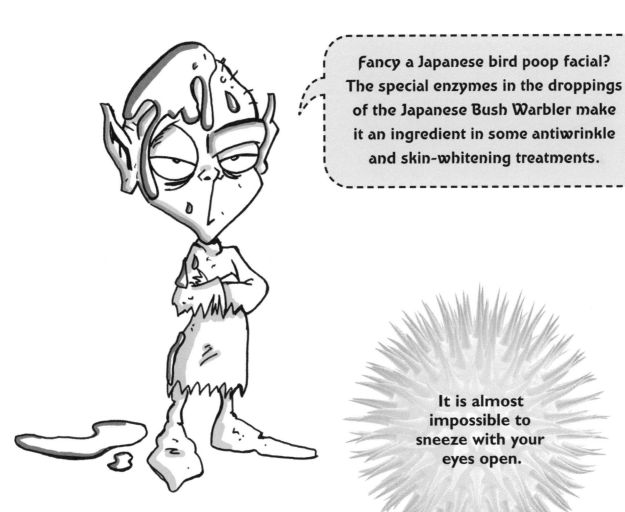

Fancy a Japanese bird poop facial? The special enzymes in the droppings of the Japanese Bush Warbler make it an ingredient in some antiwrinkle and skin-whitening treatments.

It is almost impossible to sneeze with your eyes open.

The strongest muscle in the human body is the tongue.

Some toiletries and cosmetic products contain carmine: a red substance made from crushed beetles!

Men have more nose hair than women ... and it grows longer as they get older!

The most bizarre cosmetic procedure has to be tongue-splitting: a scalpel or laser is used to cut down the middle of the tongue and give it a forked appearance. Freaky!

Your skin produces substances that are naturally antibacterial and antifungal. If it didn't, your skin would start to rot!

You have more pain sensors in your skin than any other type of sensor.

Nose-pickings are a mixture of dried mucus and what is filtered out of the air you breathe – pollen, dust, fungus, dirt, maybe the odd bug, and even tiny particles of dust from space!

Inside each eye you have a clear lens just behind your pupil. These lenses yellow slightly as you get older, affecting your perception of blue light. So if your grandma thinks your black jumper is really blue, she hasn't gone mad – it's just her eyes!

Sweat is made mainly of water, so it doesn't smell ... until it's been around a while. Once skin bacteria have had time to slurp it up and multiply, the whiff begins.

A sheet of skin can be grown from just a few of your cells. New skin is grown in special laboratories and used to replace damaged skin in a skin graft operation.

If you ate nothing but carrots, your skin would turn orange!

Your tear ducts lead from your eyes to your nose. That's why your nose runs when you cry and why you can sometimes taste eye drops.

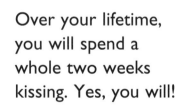

Over your lifetime, you will spend a whole two weeks kissing. Yes, you will!

Austrian man Martin Bierbauer claimed damages after he was blasted off his toilet by hailstones during a freak storm. A local spokesman admitted that blocked drains were to blame.

If you're right-handed, you will sweat most under your right arm. If you're left-handed, you're more likely to get a pit patch under your left arm!

Your wisdom teeth generally start appearing between the ages of 17 and 25.

Your belly button is the scar left from your umbilical cord. Whether it's an "innie" or an "outie" depends on the shape and size of your umbilical cord when you were born.

Horrified basketball fans thought they saw player Allan Ray get his eye poked out by an opponent during a game. In fact, his eyelid was stuck so far back that it just looked like his eyeball had come out of its socket. Still ... ouch!

Sebum is the oily stuff secreted by glands in your skin to keep it soft. The only part of your body that doesn't have any is your lips – that's why they dry out easily.

Your saliva is made up of 98 percent water.

About 80 hairs drop out of your head every day, but that still leaves you with more than 99,900 to play with while new ones grow!

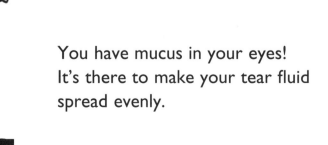

0.2 percent of the world's population has an extra finger or toe. That's 12 million people with an extra digit or two!

You have mucus in your eyes! It's there to make your tear fluid spread evenly.

Taste buds aren't just on your tongue – there are more than 2,000 of them in your throat and on the roof of your mouth.

On reaching the ripe old age of 109, British pensioner Edna McLure declared that her secret was a regular snack of bread dipped in sherry.

The 250,000 sweat glands in your feet make them one of the sweatiest parts of the body. Adults produce two whole cups of that stinky foot juice every week!

If your dead skin cells didn't drop off, after three years your skin would be as thick as an elephant's!

The koala bear is the only animal to have fingerprints almost identical to ours.

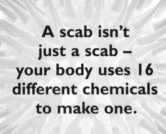

A scab isn't just a scab – your body uses 16 different chemicals to make one.

Soap works by sticking to dirt particles so that they come away from the skin. You can see the difference by washing dirty hands with just water first!

People can choose to have their bodies deep-frozen after death in case scientists of the future come up with a way of bringing them back to life … but they will have to pay around £130,000 or US$215,000 for the privilege.

The little pink lump in the corner of your eye is what remains of an extra eyelid that our predecessors had.

Each hair on your head grows for up to six years. Then it stops, hangs around for a while and eventually drops out!

Being too
hot or too cold
in bed increases
your chances
of having bad
dreams.

JewelEye is a body modification procedure available from Dutch eye clinics: the eye membrane is sliced open and a decorative platinum shape is inserted. It's not legal yet anywhere else in the world, as it's dangerous … and just crazy!

Nguyen Van Chien is one hairy Vietnamese – he hasn't had a haircut for more than 70 years!

One in three people will have a surgical operation in their lifetime.

If you ever need stitches, they could be made from catgut. Don't worry – it's actually made from sheep or goat intestines. Which is sort of better…

There are millions of things living in your mouth! Don't bother looking, though – they are microorganisms that are too small to see.

Peat bogs are very acidic and have low oxygen levels, so bodies left in them are pickled! The internal organs and facial features of bog bodies are well preserved, even if they are thousands of years old.

Each of your eyebrow hairs drops out after ten weeks.

People who lose a limb or an eye can often still feel "phantom" pains or itches in the missing part.

Sword swallowers train themselves to control the gag reflex that occurs when something touches the soft palate at the back of the mouth. If you touch it, you'll vomit … so don't try it!

Your brain weighs half as much as your skin.

"Elvis foot" is rock climber speak for a trembling foot, meaning your foot is so tired it is trembling on the rock.

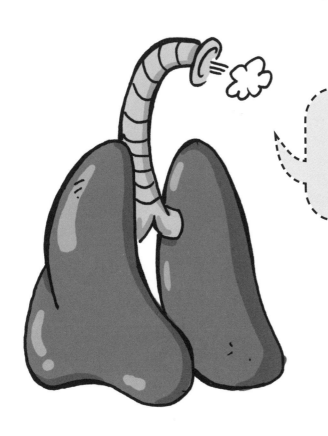

You will breathe in around 18 kg (40 lb) of dust over your lifetime – that's about 18 large bags of flour!

One in 600 people are born with kidneys that are fused together in a horseshoe shape.

Being born is really stressful! As you came into the world, you had higher levels of the stress hormone *adrenaline* than an adult has during a heart attack!

When you feel thirsty, your body is already dehydrated. It's your brain's way of telling you to get a drink, quick!

If you could remove your brain and spread it out, it would be the size of a pillowcase.

Only 4 percent of your blood is in your heart right now. The rest is racing around your body!

If you eat a lot of red beets, your urine can turn pink!

There are more cases of heart attack on a Monday than on any other day.

The brain cannot feel pain, so some brain surgery can be done while the patient is awake! The surgeon will then talk to the patient during the operation to make sure that healthy parts of the brain are not being affected.

Your funny bone is not a bone at all but a nerve that extends from your elbow to your hand.

When a dead body is decomposing, the bacteria inside it produce gases. When the gas is released from the body, it sounds like a fart!

When you have a bad tummy bug, you will eventually throw up green vomit. It is bile, which is deep down in the stomach and comes up only when nothing else is left.

There are more than 700 kinds of bacteria lurking in your intestine, including a harmless form of E. coli.

Make your hand into a fist – that's how big your heart is!

There is so much electrical activity going on in your brain that you could power a light bulb with it!

What makes poop brown is bilirubin, a substance that comes from the breakdown of old blood cells in the liver.

Your floating ribs are the last two pairs of ribs attached to your spine only.

You have an army of white blood cells to protect your body from infection. They march along your blood vessel walls, seeking out and destroying bacteria.

A really big sneeze can make you fracture a rib.

The pH level in your stomach is 1 or 2, which is more acidic than vinegar.

If you ever want to classify what you leave behind in the toilet, you should take a look at the Bristol Stool Chart. The seven types of stool listed range from "separate hard lumps, like nuts" (Type 1) to "entirely liquid" (Type 7).

More than half of your blood is made up of plasma, a pale yellow fluid containing nutrients, proteins, and waste products.

It's important to eat healthily, but take care what is in that salad – don't confuse henbane with fat-hen, the latter is fine in moderation but henbane is poisonous!

Around 51 tonnes (50 tons) of food will pass through your stomach over your lifetime.

More people die between 3am and 4am than at any other time, as this is when all the body's functions slow right down.

Modern toilets are not ideally designed for their purpose, as squatting is the best position for the body to be in when passing a stool.

There are 250 million blood cells in a tiny drop of blood.

It is your thumb that makes your hand so useful and able to grasp things securely.

When you vomit, the muscles in your stomach and intestines go into reverse: instead of pushing the food down, they push it up and out of your mouth.

When used as a food additive in luxurious desserts or drinks, gold is indicated as E175. It's just there for decoration and your body doesn't digest it – so if you eat gold, you poop gold!

British tourist Tanya Andrews developed a lump on her scalp after a holiday in Costa Rica. Her doctor confirmed that a botfly maggot had hatched from a mosquito bite and burrowed its way into her skin to hitch a ride back!

Head lice slurp blood from your scalp! Don't panic, they're so tiny that you won't feel a thing…

Bedbugs are the vampires of the pest world – they hate sunlight and prefer to venture out to bite you at night.

African tumbu flies lay their eggs in clothing. The eggs hatch on contact with human skin and the larvae burrow under the surface, creating boil-like sores to grow in.

Only female midges bite people.

You really smell with your brain not your nose. It identifies different scents.

The aggressive Australasian funnel-web spider has such sharp fangs that they can pierce through fingernails and soft shoes.

Helmintophobia is a fear of getting worms. Hands up anyone who *isn't* scared!

Harvest mite larvae are tiny orange parasites that love to eat your skin. They inject digestive juices into you to make a well of liquefied skin cells that they can then suck up. They drop off when they're done, leaving behind a nasty irritation.

A long-term Argentinian study has shown that worm infestations reduce the symptoms of the illness multiple sclerosis. The health of purposely infested sufferers improved dramatically – they just had to cope with worms for years instead!

When hotel receptionist Abbie Hawkins felt something moving on her chest while at work, she discovered a baby bat nestled inside her bra! The bat-hiding underwear had been left on the washing line the previous night.

If a wasp stings you, it's female. Ooh, nasty girl!

At just 1 mm (0.04 in) long, the tropical chigoe flea is the smallest known flea. Unlike others, it is useless at jumping.

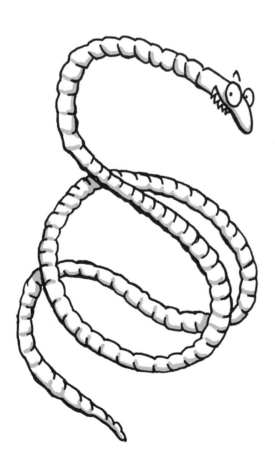

A broad tapeworm can grow in the intestine for decades, reaching a length of 10 m (33 ft). Worst of all, you may not even know you have one...

Mosquitoes hate the smell of garlic, so you can try eating some to keep them at bay. You can ward off vampires into the bargain, too!

When South African woman Elsie van Tonder tried to help a seal back into the sea, it bit off her nose! A helpful bystander picked up her nose, but it couldn't be reattached.

The common housefly carries more diseases than any other creature in the world.

In severe cases of worms, a large group can clump together in a ball and cause a blockage in the intestine or bowel.

Amoebic dysentery is caused by a parasite that kills around 70,000 people every year.
It can travel from the intestine to the liver, where it creates pus-filled abscesses.

Demodex mites are tiny parasites that live in eyebrows and eyelashes. They're very common, especially in older people. Under a microscope, they look like worms with stubby legs.

Parasites are happily living in at least 75 percent of the world's population.

Eye gnats love to slurp up tear fluid, so will try to hang around your eye area.

Many dogs and cats have worms that you can catch. If the worm infection toxocariasis is left untreated in us, it can spread to our liver, brain, and eyes.

Worms eaten in raw or undercooked fish can cause bad stomach cramps. Some people can also have a severe allergic reaction to them, known as anaphylactic shock.

Weil's disease is a serious infection that causes jaundice and kidney damage. It comes from rats' urine and is usually caught from infected water.

Black flies breed in fast-flowing rivers and spread a worm that destroys the human eye in the tropical disease river blindness.

Bedbugs and fleas can live in your house for a whole year without feeding.

Raw sewage (what goes down the toilet) is often used to fertilize fields in developing countries, but it can be full of worm eggs. When the egg-infested vegetables are eaten, worm infections are spread further.

The sting from a box jellyfish is extremely toxic and fast-acting, affecting the heart and nervous system. It can kill a person within four minutes.

The tiny scabies mite tunnels along beneath the skin in a zigzag shape, causing unbearable itching.

Girls are more likely to have head lice than boys, as they tend to have longer hair … and they do more hugging!

The female threadworm lays between 10,000 and 20,000 eggs at a time on its human host's bottom. She then spreads around a secretion that causes itching, to make the host scratch at the eggs and share them with friends…

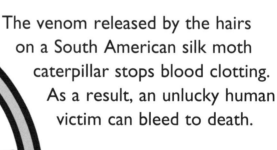

Don't think that you can spot head lice more easily in light hair – those critters can change to merge with their surroundings.

The venom released by the hairs on a South American silk moth caterpillar stops blood clotting. As a result, an unlucky human victim can bleed to death.

Maggot-like parasites were found lurking in rice about to be served at a school in Suffolk in England. Who says school dinners are yucky?

Up to 1,000 Americans each year die from allergic reactions.

Some tapeworm eggs can grow into a cyst as large as a grapefruit, filled with thousands of tapeworm heads! It's not common, so don't have nightmares…

A spitting cobra will defend itself by shooting poison into a person's eyes to make them scream in agony and leave them temporarily blind.

Sand flies spread the parasitic disease leishmaniasis through their bites. The parasites cause boils on the skin, which can last for up to a year and leave bad scars. If they find their way into the body, the parasites can also damage the internal organs.

There are more than 2,500 types of mosquito worldwide, spreading viruses and parasites that kill millions of people every year.

The sting from a stonefish will paralyze you and send you into shock.

While mosquitoes puncture the skin and suck up blood, horseflies have serrated jaws that they use to bite a chunk out of your skin so they can lap up the dribble of blood.

Dead dust mites and mite droppings are a major cause of asthma.

Gnathostoma spinigerum is a worm that wriggles around under the skin and causes an itchy, snake-shaped rash during an infestation known as creeping eruption.

One of the most common waterborne diseases is cryptosporidiosis. Tiny parasites swallowed in contaminated water hatch inside the intestine causing severe infection.

Vaccines to protect against parasitic diseases are not yet available … so we'll have to live with them for a little longer!

The wuchereria parasitic worm causes elephantiasis, a disfiguring disease where the limbs swell alarmingly and the skin thickens, becoming ulcerated.

The first insects to home in on a dead body are flies, as they like their maggots to have a moist corpse to feed on.

We're not the only ones to be bothered by head lice – even the ancient Egyptians had to put up with them.

An ear infection can be caused by an insect that has crawled into your ear and died.

Bilharzia is a flatworm infection caught by paddling or swimming in tropical lakes. It can damage the stomach, bladder, and liver, so think carefully the next time you're tempted to go for a swim on holiday…

Body lice are even worse than head lice! They live in clothing and cause intense itching.

The female chigoe flea lays her eggs by burrowing into human skin headfirst, leaving her back end sticking out. Over two weeks, she feeds on blood and lays 100 or so eggs, before dying and falling out.

Mosquitoes spread malaria when they bite and pass on saliva containing parasites. The parasites then travel through the bloodstream and multiply in the liver and red blood cells.

Malaria kills more than one million people every year.

The worst worm infection has to be the tropical Guinea worm disease. Between one and two years after drinking infected water, a spaghetti-like worm up to 100 cmm (40 in) long will pop out of a blister in the foot or leg.

The Amazonian giant centipede delivers venom through its sharp claws, so if you meet one … don't touch!

Minute pirate bugs have a beak-like proboscis (a sucking mouthpart) that they stick into the skin. Ouch!

One of the largest human flea infestations in the UK was found on a farm where more than 130 million fleas carpeted the ground!

Pretty shells can hide deadly sea snails – when touched, cone snails fire a highly poisonous harpoon so sharp that it has been known to go through wetsuits.

Some maggots love to munch away at dead flesh! This can be useul in the healing of wounds using "maggot therapy" – they leave healthy flesh alone.

New York City had a bedbug epidemic in 2007, when a record 6,889 calls were made to pest control companies. The tiny brown pests infested top hotels, hospitals, cinemas, and schools, as well as homes.

Each female head louse lives for a month and can lay up to 150 eggs in that time.

You have at least a million dust mites crawling around your mattress and pillow, gobbling up all your old skin cells.

A man known as Snake Manu loves a bit of "snake flossing" – he puts slim snakes, including deadly cobras, up his nose and passes them out through his mouth.

Horseflies in West Africa spread the loa loa worm through their bites. The infection is also known as African eye worm, as the sufferer may feel the worms wriggling across their eyeballs. Eek!

Fluffy puss caterpillars look good enough to stroke, but poisonous spines are lurking under their soft hair. When touched, the spines lodge painfully in the skin, causing numbness, blisters, and a rash.

Threadworm eggs can survive for up to three weeks outside the human body.

Sweat bees are so called because they love the salt in your sweat! Don't worry – their sting is almost painless compared to that of other bees.

A zoonosis is an infectious disease that can be transferred between animals and people, such as bird flu.

A viper bites on a limb can be so harmful that even if the victim doesn't die, they may have to have the affected limb amputated.

It takes only two months for one pregnant flea to become an infestation of one million fleas.

The most common flea worldwide is the cat flea … which is just as happy sucking human blood, if it can't find a cat.

One type of roundworm, that can be caught by eating undercooked pork, starts off in the intestine but then wriggles off to live in the body's muscles.

A flea can live in your house for up to two years ... if you don't catch it first!

The best reason to check for head lice is the saying that "what goes in must come out" – if they're feeding on your blood, they're pooping in your hair!

Botfly eggs are spread by mosquitoes and hatch on contact with human skin. The maggots get comfy under the skin's surface and cling on with hooked spines, making them difficult to remove.

The paralyzing venom of the blue ring octopus is more toxic to humans than that of any land animal.

A bite from a wheel bug causes agony that can last for up to six hours.

The largest beetle in New Zealand is the Huhu and it can give you a nasty nip with its strong jaws! It also has sharp hooks on its long legs and antennae, so its other name is the "haircutter" – if one gets tangled in your hair, it has to be cut out with scissors!

If a woman has a worm infection, she can pass it on to her baby through her breast milk.

After 40 years of keeping bees, Michael Lynch from Derbyshire, England, became allergic to bee stings.

Head lice are sensitive to heat and will abandon the head of someone with a fever.

Greedy young head lice can die from overfeeding, as their tiny guts spring a leak if they drink too much of your blood.

A jellyfish that is washed up on the shore can still sting you if its tentacles are wet.

Ticks plunge barbs into the skin of their host to keep them anchored in place. That's why they're difficult to remove!

A man who went to a Dubai hospital with a sore eye was shocked to discover that he had a 10-cm (4-in)-long worm inside it! Once removed, the parasite was identified as a canine heart worm, which doesn't normally infest humans.

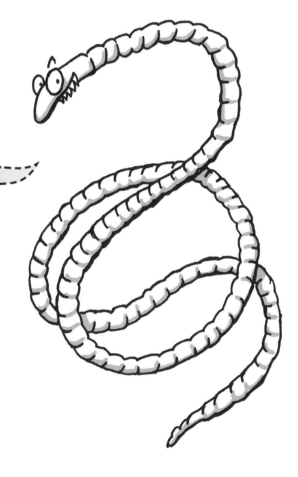

A flea that has lived on a cat with tapeworm can then pass on tapeworm eggs when it bites a human.

Leeches carry viruses, bacteria, and parasites from their previous hosts and pass them on to subsequent victims.

An emerging Guinea worm makes the skin feel as if it's burning, so sufferers often soak their limbs in the nearest river to soothe them. The worm then releases hundreds of thousands of larvae into the water and the cycle begins again.

A woman who tried on some jeans in a shop in Okinawa, Japan, ended up leaving in an ambulance! She was stung by a scorpion that was hiding inside the jeans.

Mosquitoes are attracted to the carbon dioxide that you breathe out, so there's no escape!

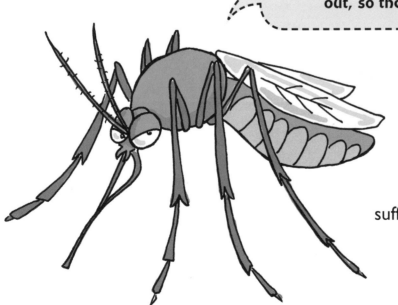

Body lice were a huge problem for soldiers in World Wars I and II. They caused terrible itching and also spread trench fever, a disease with agonizing head, eye, and leg pains that put sufferers out of action for a month.

Liver flukes are parasitic flatworms that can be caught through contaminated water or meat. They slurp blood in the liver, causing ulcers and severe digestive problems.

A tick's saliva contains a numbing substance, which is why you can't feel it biting!

Three people were stung to death by bees when a truck loaded with beehives crashed and overturned in the Jilin province of China.

One nasty symptom of giardiasis is foul, sulphuric burps that can be so bad they induce vomiting! The infection is caused by a parasite that has tentacle-like limbs.

The tiny Irukandji jellyfish has a highly toxic sting that can give an unsuspecting swimmer agonizing cramps and cause a rapid rise in heart rate, sweating, and vomiting.

Head lice have little stumpy legs, so they can't jump. They don't walk very well on flat surfaces, either, so if one drops out of your hair, it is easy to catch!

More than a billion people have a hookworm infection, which means they have tiny blood-sucking worms living in their intestine. All those hookworms suck a total of 10 million l (22 million pt) of blood a day!

Biologist Mike Leahy is so committed to his work that he volunteered to swallow a tapeworm for research purposes. By the time he got rid of it, the worm was 3 m (10 ft) long!

Forensic entomologists examine the maggots and beetles on corpses to work out the time of a person's death.

A bite from a black widow spider doesn't hurt until about half an hour later ... when the swelling, sweating, headaches, and vomiting start.

Stingrays have a barbed stinger on their tail, which whips up to puncture any creature perceived as a threat. This isn't normally fatal – Australian celebrity Steve Irwin died because the stingray's barb pierced his heart as he swam above it.

Dust mites love a bit of dandruff and like to take up residence in a flaky scalp!

The only way to get a Guinea worm out of the skin safely is by wrapping it around a stick very ... very ... slowly, which can take up to a month!

Female fleas are bigger than males.

The tropical virus chikungunya is spread by mosquito bites and arrived in Europe for the first time in 2007. Symptoms include fever, joint pain, and a severe headache.

Ticks can spread Rocky Mountain spotted fever, originally known as "black measles" – it is a severe illness that causes fever, muscle pain, headache, and a rash, and occurs all over the Americas.

There are 2,000 types of flea on the planet.

The bite of a fire ant feels like a nasty burn on your skin and turns into an itchy white blister.

1.5 billion people around the world have *ascariasis*, an infection in which earthworm-like parasites can grow as long as 30 cm (12 in) inside the intestine.

If you find an empty nest close to your house, ask someone to get rid of it or the hungry bird mites left behind will come inside at night to seek out your blood!

In Tibet sticking your tongue out at someone is regarded as a friendly greeting.

Female head lice use a very sticky protein to glue their eggs on to hair strands. You can shake your head, wash your hair, or swim underwater ... those eggs won't budge!

Being stung on the finger by a scorpion will send shooting pains all the way up your arm.

Some leeches just won't let go! One Hong Kong woman had to have one surgically removed from her nostril when it clung on for weeks after she washed her face in an infested stream. The nose invader was 5 cm (2 in) long.

Cellulitis is a skin reaction that can follow an insect bite: the area around the bite swells alarmingly and has to be treated with antibiotics.

Forty percent of children under the age of ten in the UK will get a threadworm infection.

Lionfish have venomous fin spines that cause agonizing stings, nausea, breathing difficulties, and convulsions.

You don't have to swallow hookworms to catch them – they can bore through the skin on your feet!

In 2004, a South African man purposely released deadly puff adders into the bank that repossessed his car. A cleaner was bitten and the man was charged with attempted murder.

Threadworm eggs are so small that you can't see them. They can float through the air, so you can catch worms if the eggs zoom up your nose when you breathe in!

A severe bout of malaria can send a sufferer into a coma.

Some tick saliva is neurotoxic, which means it can affect the nervous system and cause tick paralysis.

Head lice prefer clean hair to dirty hair, as it's easier to grip on to.

Rat fleas spread the deadly disease bubonic plague. Although it's rare these days, the illness killed around one-third of the population of 14th-century Europe, when it was known as The Black Death.

Intestinal myiasis means maggots in the stomach! The maggots can be swallowed in infected food and cause stomach pains, but are eventually digested by gastric juices.

Hookworm larvae can penetrate the skin, causing itchy lumps that look like bites.

Badgers may seem cuddly, but they have razor-sharp teeth and they're not afraid to use them! After a badger attacked five people in Evesham, England, one man needed plastic surgery to repair the injuries on his legs and arm.

Pediculosis is the name for being infested with lice.

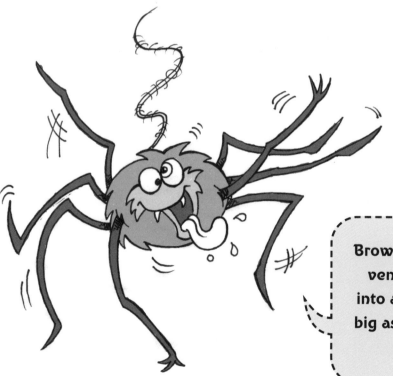

Brown recluse spiders have necrotic venom, which makes a bite turn into an ulcerous sore that can be as big as 25 cm (10 in) across, and take months to heal.

The most painful ant bite comes from the bullet ant. Some Amazonian tribesmen purposely put them on their skin during rituals to test their bravery.

The maggots used in maggot therapy eat dead flesh, but those of the screw-worm fly eat healthy flesh. If they infest a wound, they burrow in and destroy the healthy tissue around it, making the wound far worse.

Parts of the pufferfish are poisonous enough to kill an adult human. Only specially trained chefs are able to prepare it for cooking.

A bad infestation of threadworm can cause *appendicitis*.

Head lice eggs are brown, but turn white once hatched.

The Congo floor maggot sucks human blood! It comes out at night looking for people sleeping on the ground.

Up to forty million Americans have threadworm at any one time.

Pitohui birds have a sting in their tail! Their vibrant feathers release a toxin, so touching them will make your fingers numb.

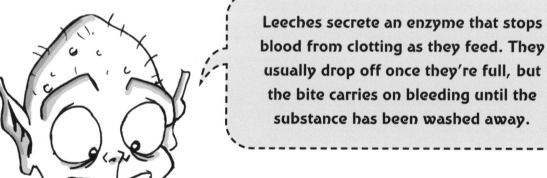

Leeches secrete an enzyme that stops blood from clotting as they feed. They usually drop off once they're full, but the bite carries on bleeding until the substance has been washed away.

In large numbers, hookworms can suck so much blood from the small intestine that they make the sufferer feel absolutely exhausted.

After five days of having his arm trapped under a fallen boulder, American mountaineer Aron Ralston had to take drastic action: he cut off his arm with a penknife.

St Louis barber, Bill Black, saved the hair clippings swept from his floor and used them to make vests, shirts, ties, and even a bikini! Itchy!

During an argument about a fence, British pensioner June Iddon whacked her the man next door with a spade and broke his arm.

Following his arrest for drink driving, American José Cruz was also charged with assault when he farted on a police officer. In his statment, the officer complained how smelly it was.

Australian performance artist Stelarc had a human ear grafted on to his forearm in the name of art. He can literally turn a deaf ear to anyone who annoys him!

A Chinese farmer was unconscious for 11 hours after catching his finger on a needle filled with a knock-out drug meant for a deer.

When Indian man Dharmendra Singh smokes a cigarette, the smoke comes out of his ears.

Australian doctor Barry Marshall insisted that stomach ulcers were not caused by stress or spicy foods but by the bacterium Helicobacter pylori. He proved his point by swallowing a Petri dish full of it!

Norwegian footballer Svein Grondalen had to miss an international match through injury after crashing into a moose while out jogging. Those beasts are difficult to spot...

One of singer Screamin' Jay Hawkins' songs was called "Constipation Blues"...

British entertainer Mr Methane describes himself as "the world's only full-time performing flatulist" – people pay to hear him fart tunes!

Some cultures have a tradition of earlobe stretching: people wear heavy earrings that can weigh up to 500 g (1 lb) and hang them from huge holes in their earlobes.

Chinese man Li Jianping has grown the fingernails on his left hand for more than 15 years. Their total length is more than 1 m (3 ft), so he avoids busy places in case he breaks one.

Reclusive billionaire Howard Hughes had such a phobia of germs that his staff had to cover his cutlery handles with layers of tissue paper and cellophane.

When Italian police investigated complaints against dentist-from-hell Alvaro Perez, they discovered he had been using a regular power drill on his patients and had no dental qualifications.

Some African cultures use *scarification* to decorate their skin with patterns of raised scars.

A Polish car thief who left his false teeth at the crime scene was caught when police matched them to his dental records.

Fast food addicts Tom and Kerry Watts celebrated their marriage with a giant burger that contained the equivalent of 100 quarter pounders!

American Kevin Kearney was kitesurfing in a tropical storm on a Florida beach, when he was picked up by the wind and smashed into a street some distance away.

Body modification fan Erl Van Aken had a flap of skin on his stomach formed into a kind of handle shape that he could put his finger through. Why? Just because!

After American cyclist Robert Evans was hit by a car in a hit-and-run accident, he was hit by a train on his way home from the hospital. What a bad day...

A Chinese man had to take his girlfriend to hospital when she swallowed the engagement ring he had hidden in her cake.

A one-month-old baby was rushed to hospital after his grandmother misunderstood the instructions and sent him through the hand luggage X-ray machine at Los Angeles airport.

Carpenter Patrick Lawler suffered blurred vision and toothache after his nail gun backfired and a nail struck his face. An X-ray six days later showed a second 10-cm (4-in) nail embedded in his brain!

German fishermen got a shocking catch from the River Rhine – a severed arm! Police thought it belonged to a man as it was hairy.

Dutch artist Joanneke Meester made a tiny pistol from a piece of her own skin to protest against rising levels of violence.

When two American ice hockey players collided at a match, the skate of one accidentally sliced the jugular vein of the goalkeeper. The sight of blood gushing across the ice made three spectators have heart attacks. The goalkeeper didn't feel too good either!

One medieval treatment for a skin infection was to rub cow dung on it.

Zombies really do exist! Haitian witch doctors called bokors can use plant-based drugs to make a person appear to be dead, then revive them and keep them under their control.

Estonians have an age-old saying: if you point at a rainbow, your finger will fall off.

Hawaiian Kala Kaiwi has used wooden discs to stretch the holes in his earlobes to an eye-watering 10 cm (4 in) across.

French Admiral Gaspard de Coligny found a novel use for his bushy beard – he kept his toothpicks in it!

The annual Mooning Amtrak event involves thousands of people showing their bottoms to passing trains in California. The organizers especially welcome decorated and obese butts!

When American recluse Homer Collyer died, police and workmen cleared rubbish from his junk-filled house for two weeks before they found the body of his brother, Langley Collyer.

A Swiss thief whose finger was cut off by broken glass was caught when police found the finger at the crime scene and matched its print with their records.

British man Richard Ross was holding a nail between his lips while doing DIY, when he inhaled it! His ribs had to be broken for the lung surgery necessary to remove it.

Several people have been injured or drowned trying to go over the edge of Niagara Falls. (And it's illegal, anyway.)

When a Chinese boy had an operation to correct a limp, the surgeons lengthened the wrong leg! The confusion arose when the boy was on his back for the assessment but on his stomach for the surgery.

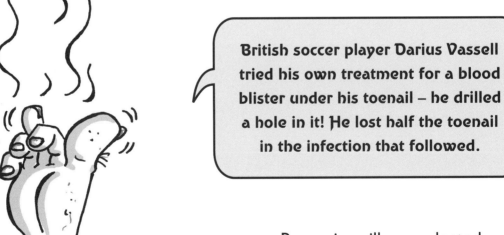

British soccer player Darius Vassell tried his own treatment for a blood blister under his toenail – he drilled a hole in it! He lost half the toenail in the infection that followed.

Romanian villagers elected Neculai Ivascu as their mayor for a second term … even though he died just before the election.

The Si La people of Laos have an old tradition of painting their teeth: men have red teeth and women have black.

Australian rugby player Jamie Ainscough suffered a severe arm infection that puzzled doctors. The mystery was solved when an X-ray revealed an opponent's tooth embedded under his skin!

New Zealand man William Singalargh was arrested for using a hedgehog as an offensive weapon – he threw it at a youth, causing scratches and puncture wounds.

When javelin thrower Tero Pitkamaki slipped in his run-up during a competition in Rome, his javelin flew off into French long jumper Salim Sdiri, damaging his liver and right kidney.

British angler Peter Hodge wanted to be fed to the fish when he died, so his ashes were mixed with fish food and he was thrown into a river.

After Czech President Vaclav Claus had a hip replacement operation, a police investigation began – when his original hip was put up for sale on an internet auction site!

Just some of the items awaiting collection at Transport For London's Lost Property Office include false teeth, breast implants, false limbs, and a bag containing two human skulls.

American Don Gorske has scoffed 23,000 Big Macs in 36 years. He even kept the receipts to prove it!

Having scored the winning goal against Ecuador in a 2006 World Cup match, England captain David Beckham threw up on the pitch.

One million people each decade are killed in natural disasters.

Singer Bantcho Bantchevsky jumped off a balcony and killed himself during the interval of an opera at New York's Metropolitan Opera House.

English sportsman Ian Greig went for an X-ray when he injured his hand during a match … and cut his head open on the machine as he stood up, needing stitches!

American politician Stan Jones drank a solution made with silver as a home remedy, in the belief that it would boost his immune system. He felt great, but his skin turned permanently blue-silver!

American George Chandler narrowly avoided serious brain damage when the nail gun he was using went off accidentally and nailed his hat to his head. The nail pierced his brain but was safely removed.

Pilgrims to the Tirupati temple in India give their hair as a sacrifice. The temple's 600 barbers shave thousands of visitors every day.

A man who was diving for golf balls in a Florida lake had his arm broken by an attacking alligator. He was saved by a nearby golfer, who whacked the alligator with his club.

Three military band members were injured when a skydiver crashed into them at around 80 km (50 miles) per hour during a ceremony in Kansas, USA.

Entertainer Roy Horn was seriously injured when a tiger he used in his act gripped him in its teeth and ran off with him.

Women of the Ethiopian Surma tribe have an old tradition of putting a clay disk in the bottom lip to stretch it out. The lower teeth have to be removed first, though...

A World War II veteran who had been blind for 64 years had his sight miraculously restored when he was butted in the head by a horse!

The USA has three body farms – research establishments where dead bodies are left to decay in various situations, even in the boot of a car! Scientists study the decomposition process, using the information to help with murder investigations.

Your farts could be put to good use! Inventors Michael Zanakis and Philip Femano thought so – they patented a fart-powered toy rocket in 2005.

Plugged-up sweat glands cause prickly heat rash in hot weather – fresh sweat gets trapped and forms a prickling, itchy rash of tiny blisters.

After 30 years of smelling like stale fish, a 41 year-old Australian woman finally had her rare disorder diagnosed: trimethylaminuria, a syndrome and affects the smell of sweat, breath, and urine.

Many beauty salons now offer fish pedicures: just dip your feet in the water full of garra rufa fish and they nibble away all the flaky skin!

People travel from all over the world to enter the annual tongue-tingling Nettle Eating Championships in Dorset, England.

Brazilian priest Adelir de Carli attached himself to 1,000 helium-filled balloons in a publicity stunt that went tragically wrong. He was blown out to sea and only the lower half of his body was found several weeks later.

Chinese man Ru Anting can write on paper with water squirted from his eyes! He decided to hone his eye-spraying skill for entertainment when he lost his factory job.

British reptile shop employee Lee Thompson almost died after he was bitten by an adder in his shop ... but made a full recovery and decided to keep the venomous snake as a pet!

Scientists have worked out that you have a 300 million to one chance of dying from a shark attack.

An Indian man was so desperate to go to the 2007 Cricket World Cup in the West Indies that he sold one of his kidneys to pay for the trip.

A man was banned from a pub in Scotland ... because he kept doing smelly farts!

The highlight of the year in the Japanese city of Shibukawa is the Belly Button Festival. People dance in the streets with faces painted on their stomachs.

When British man John Stirling accidentally sawed off his arm with a chainsaw, he calmly asked his friend next door to help and sat on a stool till the ambulance arrived! Meanwhile, the friend packed the arm in a bag of frozen pastries so that it could be reattached.

Artist Marco Evaristti held a dinner party and served meatballs made with his own liposuction fat! How tasty...

At the age of four, Australian Sam Carpenter caught his hand in a meat mincer at his father's butcher's shop. Half of his arm had to be amputated, but he went on to become a professional Australian rules football player.

A patient in a Belgrade hospital was alarmed to discover that two surgeons had started a fight during his operation! The assistant surgeon completed the procedure instead.

Austrian hunter Hans Biedermeier accidentally shot himself as he was shaking the snow out of his rifle during a hunting trip.

An 80-year-old Chinese man agreed to have his hair and beard washed for the first time in 23 years. Twelve relatives and friends spent five hours getting all the grime out of his 2-m (6-ft)-long matted locks and 1.5 m (5-ft)-long beard!

Argentinian artist Nicola Constantino used fat removed from her body to make 100 soaps and two sculptures.

Some ear infections make you throw up! Viruses that affect the inner ear can alter your sense of balance and make you feel seasick.

Chinese man Zhang Yinming can snort milk up through his nose and squirt it out of his eyes up to 2 m (6 ft) away.

Nasal polyps are fleshy growths in the nostril that can affect the sense of smell – a big one can be the size of a grape!

Himalayan Apatani tribeswomen used to enlarge their nostrils with 2.5-cm (1-in)-wide circular nose plugs.

When German man Udo Ried dropped a kitchen knife on his foot and chopped off a toe, his cat Fritz ran off with it as he hopped around phoning for an ambulance!

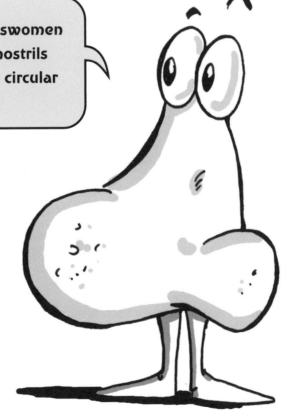

Body piercing fans like to stick jewelry in their nipples, on the back of their necks, through their tongues, and in the soft bit between the eyes. Ouch!

Carbuncles are skin abscesses that can be as big as golf balls and ooze pus from one or two openings – and they're contagious!

Entropion is a condition in which the eyelid turns inward and rubs against the eyeball. If left untreated, it causes an ulcer and can lead to blindness.

Police in Soweto, South Africa, had to deal with a series of assaults ... by giant rats! They were nesting in old cars and attacking people who passed by.

Indian artist Shihan Hussaini painted 56 portraits of politician Jayalalitha for her 56th birthday. As a personal touch, he used some of his own blood as the paint.

When soccer player Paulo Diogo tried to jump over a barrier during a goal celebration, his wedding ring got caught and he lost the top half of his finger. The referee even gave him a yellow card for wasting time!

American playwright Tennessee Williams choked to death on a bottle top.

One way to pass the time in some parts of Africa is to take part in kudu dung spitting. The It involves spitting pellets of antelope dung as far as you can!

Native American body modification fan "Stalking Cat" had tiger-stripe body tattoos, surgically elongated ears, and facial implants so that he could screw in whiskers.

After accidentally swallowing a toothbrush, an Indian man endured a whole week of agonizing stomach pains before finally seeing a doctor.

For his "Only You" exhibition, Uruguayan artist Carlos Capelán created collages made from his toenail clippings.

American celebrity Jocelyn Wildenstein has spent around £2.4 million (US$4 million), on cosmetic surgery to look more like a cat, to please her husband who loved big cats.

Obstipation is severe, agonizing constipation.

A streaker leaped over a fence on to the pitch at an Australian rules football match ... and managed to knock himself out when he landed!

One symptom of scarlet fever is strawberry tongue – the tongue swells up and turns bright red, making it look like a strawberry.

Staff at an acupuncture clinic locked up and went home for the night when there was still someone in a treatment room! The woman had to remove the needles herself and call for help.

A Mexican man put hooks through his upper body and dangled by them from a tree to protest against discrimination against people with tattoos and piercings.

When medics were called to take Florida woman Gayle Grinds to hospital, they found that she was stuck to her couch – after spending six years on it, the obese woman's skin had fused with the fabric.

At the age of 15, British girl Jean Burgess decided she would never have her hair cut again. When she reached 55, her hair was 1.65 m (5 ft 6 in) long and took more than two hours to comb!

A British pensioner had to take her dog to the vet when she realized it had eaten her false teeth! The dog had a three-hour operation to have them removed. A quick rinse and they were as good as new…

Police had to guard a Bangladesh hospital after 15,000 people tried to get inside to see the two-headed baby that had been born there in August 2008.

A study of British people commuting on public transport showed that one in four of them had bacteria from excrement on their hands. That's poop germs to the rest of us. Ewww!

When a Polish man criticized the country's president, Lech Kaczynski, during a police check, he was asked to show more respect. He replied with a loud fart and was promptly arrested!

American sideshow performer Enigma has had surgery to give him horns on his head. He has a jigsaw puzzle tattoo that covers his whole body, too.

It takes just 60 seconds for Indian man Vijayakanth to pass a nylon thread through his tear duct and out through his mouth.

British performance artist Mark McGowan staged "The Withered Arm" protest against war, when he strapped his raised arm to a street light for two weeks – it drained the blood from his arm and possibly caused muscle damage.

Hindus who attend the Malaysian Thaipusam festival stick skewers through their skin as part of the celebrations.

An American company has marketed Subtle Butt – fabric strips that stick inside your underwear to neutralize farty smells. If only they were soundproof, too!

A damaged cornea can be replaced in a straightforward cornea transplant operation, but the new cornea has to come from a fresh corpse.

Puerto Rican man Angel Medina's final wish was to stay standing for his three-day wake. His corpse was embalmed in an upright position and topped off with a Yankees baseball cap for relatives to say their last goodbyes.

Australian Graham Barker has 30 years' worth of his belly button fluff saved in storage jars.

Italian artist Piero Manzoni filled 90 small tins with his own poop for a 1961 exhibition. They were sold to art buyers at a price equal to their weight in gold!

Nose mucus is normally clear and runny, but if you have a bacterial infection it will turn thick and yellow, or even green!

Nine years after being blinded in an accident, a British man got his sight back when he was struck by lightning.

An Iranian woman's grounds for divorce were that her husband was just disgusting – he hadn't washed for over a year!

In 2002, Anatomist Gunther von Hagens carried out the first public autopsy for 170 years. Over 500 people paid to watch him slice and saw a man's body, before removing its internal organs. The cancerous bladder that killed Italian biologist Lazzaro Spallanzani is on display in a museum in Pavia.

The deadly poison strychnine causes dramatic muscle spasms throughout the body until the back arches and breathing stops.

Brazilian-born Elaine Davidson is the world's most pierced woman. She has more than 5,000 piercings and can put her little finger through a hole in her tongue.

A canoeist who stopped to help a fisherman pull a shark from an African river ended up needing 50 stitches in his arm when it bit him!

British hypnotist Bernadine Coady hypnotized herself so that she could have an operation on her knee without being made unconscious.

The deadly Ebola virus makes sufferers throw up thick, black vomit.

English artist Marc Quinn made a model of his head from 4 l (8 pt) of his own deep-frozen blood. The blood for the work, entitled *Self*, was collected over five months.

Several people have donated their bodies to anatomist Gunther von Hagens so that he can plastinate (preserve and dissect) them for his Body Worlds exhibitions.

Canadian skater Jessica Dube needed plastic surgery after her partner's skate sliced her face during a side-by-side spin in a competition routine.

Soccer player Darren Barnard tore a knee ligament when he slipped on a puddle of his puppy's pee in his kitchen.

British teenager Ianthe Fullagar screamed so loudly when she found out she'd won millions on the lottery that her frightened dog jumped up and bit her on the behind!

When a woman died in the economy section of a plane shortly after it took off, she was moved to first class for the remainder of the long flight. Surely there are better ways of getting an upgrade…

Pickled human organs were found among the 103 tonnes (101 tons) of junk removed from the Collyer brothers' house in Harlem, USA.

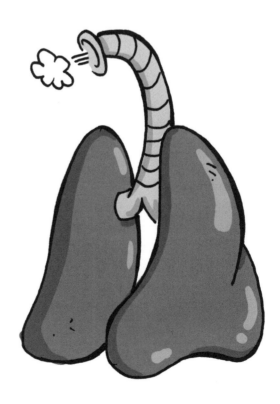

American Matt Gone hated his birthmarks so much that he had his body covered in a pattern of squares to hide them. That's 500 hours' worth of tattoos!

Ancient Egyptians cleaned their teeth with powder made from crushed ox hooves and burned eggshells.

French medical student Ernest Duchesne discovered the bacteria-destroying properties of mildewy growths after seeing that musty, mildewy saddles cured sores on horses. This was 30 years before Alexander Fleming took all the glory!

Smallpox killed 400,000 Europeans every year in the 18th century.

Ancient Greek ruler Histiaeus found a novel way of getting a secret message to his son-in-law – he tattooed it on a slave's shaven head and waited for the hair to grow back before sending him off on his mission.

Being crushed by an elephant was a common form of execution in ancient Asia.

Pus is a gooey yellow cocktail of dead cells, bacteria, proteins, and white blood cells.

Bobby Leach was the first man to go over Niagara Falls in a barrel, surviving multiple injuries. He went out with less of a fanfare, dying from gangrene after slipping on some orange peel.

A popular Victorian beauty treatment contained arsenic, vinegar, and chalk. What's a little arsenic poisoning if you have perfect skin?

One of the most desirable jobs in a medieval royal household was Groom of the Stool. Wiping the king's bottom was included in the job description!

In ancient Greece, a sneeze was believed to be a good sign from the gods.

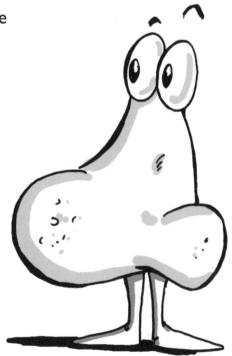

Pliny the Elder, an ancient Roman, said eating lion fat was a cure for epilepsy. If there were no lions around, sufferers could always try one of his other suggestions – dried camel's brain in vinegar!

Ancient Egyptian physicians used acacia thorns as needles when they stitched up wounds.

Nine people died in the 1814 London beer flood, when thousands of gallons of beer gushed through the streets from ruptured brewery vats.

An ancient criminal punishment was to sew the condemned person inside a rotting animal skin and tie it to a tree. The criminal would then be eaten alive by the first hungry creature that came along.

Richard the Lionheart died from an arrow wound that became gangrenous.

Greek philosopher Aristotle believed that nose mucus came from the brain.

American trainee doctor Stubbins Firth was so convinced that *yellow fever* wasn't infectious that he drank a sufferer's "fresh black vomit" – he escaped the deadly disease even though it is contagious (but transmitted through blood).

The Native American Mandan tribe used to keep the skulls of their dead, arranging them in a circle near their village.

Eighteenth-century toothpaste recipes included burned bread and dragon's blood. It's not quite so gruesome as it sounds – dragon's blood was a red plant resin.

The dentures belonging to American President George Washington were made from hippopotamus teeth.

It was against ancient Roman law to dissect human bodies; physicians of the time had to make do with dead pigs and monkeys for their research.

Medieval soldiers used a *trebuchet* to catapult things over castle walls at their enemies – including severed heads!

Greedy Swedish monarch King Adolf Frederick's biggest meal consisted of lobster, caviar, kippers, and cabbage, followed by 14 servings of dessert. It was to be his last – he died soon after of digestion problems.

British Prime Minister William Gladstone lost his left forefinger in an accident while reloading a gun.

The terrifying 15th-century warrior Pier Gerlofs Donia was known for his ability to chop off several enemies' heads with one swing of his great sword.

Incredibly Strange Body Quiz

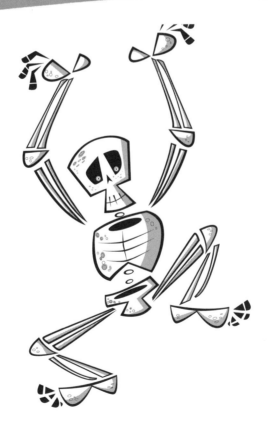

BODY QUIZ 1

TOO STINKY!

1 Why is your poop a yucky brown?

a) most food is brown
b) digestive bile makes it brown
c) to disguise it in the wild

2 If you eat lots of roughage in your diet, what will it do to your toilet habits?

a) make you poop more
b) block you up
c) give you the runs

3 Which bizarre liquid was used as a substitute for blood plasma in World War II?

a) lemonade
b) grape juice
c) coconut water

4 Before false teeth were invented, what did rich people use as replacements?

a) goats' teeth
b) teeth from human corpses
c) metal nails

5 What might a pinworm do to your bottom?

a) suck blood from it
b) chew off any pimples
c) lay its eggs there

6 Which of these body parts keeps on growing for your whole life?

a) your tongue
b) your eyeballs
c) your ears

1 SLIME BONUS POINT

7 Nose mucus is normally clear but what happens if you get a bacterial infection?

a) it turns black
b) it turns green
c) it dries up

8 What is it impossible to do on the moon because there is no gravity?

a) burp
b) wee
c) swallow

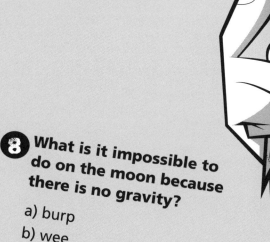

9 How fast can you make a sneeze travel into someone else's face? (Don't try this!)

a) 16 km (10 mph)
b) 160 kmph (100 mph)
c) 1,600 kmph (1,000 mph)

1 SLIME BONUS POINT

10 What do we make in our stomachs that is deadly outside our bodies?

a) cyanide
b) hydrochloric acid
c) arsenic

Answers on page 102

BODY QUIZ 2

1 If your vomit is soupy rather than lumpy when it comes out, what does that tell you?

  a) you've only just eaten
  b) you ate a while ago
  c) you had soup for dinner

2 Which mouth condition gives you a white hairy fungus on your tongue?

  a) foot and mouth disease
  b) cold sores
  c) oral thrush

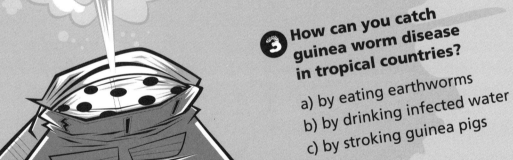

3 How can you catch guinea worm disease in tropical countries?

  a) by eating earthworms
  b) by drinking infected water
  c) by stroking guinea pigs

4 Which of these vegetables is most likely to make you fart?

  a) baked beans
  b) sweetcorn
  c) peas

1 SLIME BONUS POINT

5 Which of these stinky foods will really make your sweat pong?

a) cheese
b) fish
c) garlic

6 Your bones are alive! What is the hard part made of?

1 SLIME BONUS POINT

a) mostly collagen
b) mostly minerals
c) mostly carbon

7 Which animal has fingerprints almost identical to a human?

a) koala bear
b) polar bear
c) grizzly bear

8 Hookworm is a parasite that feeds off your blood. Where does it live?

a) in your gut
b) in your liver
c) in your lungs

9 When you are born, you have 306 bones. As an adult you have 206 bones. Why?

a) some bones dissolve
b) some bones fuse together
c) some bones crumble apart

10 If you have mites (tiny spider-like creatures) on your body, where are they likely to live?

a) in your eyebrows
b) between your toes
c) on your gums

Answers on page 102

BODY QUIZ 3

1 In most people, which part of their body is the sweatiest?

a) their palms
b) their underarms
c) their feet

2 You have tiny touch sensors under your skin. What do they look like?

a) bunches of bananas
b) squashed onions
c) cabbage leaves

3 Where does acupuncture, the treatment of sticking needles into a person's body, come from?

a) Iceland
b) Thailand
c) China

4 About how long does it take for food to reach your stomach after you've swallowed it?

a) seven seconds
b) seven minutes
c) seven hours

5 What makes sticky earwax drop out of your ear?

a) tiny earmites push it out
b) chewing and yawning
c) extremely loud noises

6 When was the first set of porcelain false teeth created?

a) 1244
b) 1744
c) 1944

1 SLIME BONUS POINT

7 What hideous thing do men do, but not women, as they get older?

a) let off smelly farts
b) pick their nose
c) grow ear hair

8 How many teaspoons of bacteria do you have living inside your body?

a) 1
b) 6
c) 16

9 Why do your feet get all wrinkly in the bath?

a) dead skin cells swell up
b) sweat makes your skin loose
c) the blood drains out of them

1 SLIME BONUS POINT

10 What does vomit contain that makes it taste so vile?

a) rotten food
b) liver bile
c) stale urine

Answers on page 102

BODY QUIZ 4

1 How far would the amount of toilet paper Americans use to wipe their bums in one day stretch?

a) once round the world
b) nine times round the world
c) to the moon and back

2 Which city's homes and hotels were infested by bed bugs in 2007?

a) London
b) Paris
c) New York

3 Up to how long can a blood-sucking flea live in your house if you don't catch it?

a) two years
b) two months
c) two days

1 SLIME BONUS POINT

4 What is your brain mostly made up of?

a) fat
b) muscle
c) water

5 Where is the skin thinnest on your body?

a) your lips
b) your bum cheeks
c) your eyelids

6 What revolting trick can 85 percent of the population do with their tongue?

a) curl it into a tube
b) poke it up their nose
c) tie it in a knot

7 Roundworms live inside you and feed off your intestines. How do you catch them?

a) by eating food with poop germs
b) by eating earthworms
c) by eating smelly cheese

8 What is a nickname for painful leg muscle cramps?

a) patty panda
b) mickey mouse
c) charley horse

9 What is the name for a large abscess on the skin that oozes pus from one or two holes?

1 SLIME BONUS POINT

a) a pimple
b) a boil
c) a carbuncle

10 How long was the longest tapeworm ever found inside a human?

a) 3 m (10 ft)
b) 33 m (108 ft)
c) 330 m (1,082 ft)

Answers on page 102

BODY QUIZ 5

1 What is exploding head syndrome?

a) a really bad headache
b) a cracked skull
c) a crashing sound in your ears

2 According to a UK survey, what did one in four people have on their hands?

a) dried-up snot
b) poop germs
c) stale urine

3 How many 50-g (1.7-oz) bars of chocolate do you need to eat in one go for the toxic chemicals in them to kill you?

a) 25
b) 205
c) 2,005

4 A healthy liver is reddish brown and smooth. What is a diseased liver like?

a) black and bruised
b) yellow and knobbly
c) green and shrunken

5 What is the medical term for picking your nose and eating the bogey?

a) mucophagy
b) bogeyitus
c) noseaphobia

1 SLIME BONUS POINT

REALLY HORRID!

6 What is the name of the infection where fungus feeds on dead skin between your toes?

a) athlete's foot
b) shoe scab
c) foot rot

7 Frenchman Michel Lotito had an unusually strong stomach. What was he known for eating?

a) insects
b) bicycles
c) newspaper

9 Some people have a fossette. What do you think it is?

a) a knobbly cabbage-like ear
b) a bobbly red nose
c) a dimple on your chin

8 What is the soft spongy material in the middle of your bones called?

a) bone jelly
b) bone marrow
c) bone squash

10 If you laid out an average adult man's skin flat, what would it cover?

a) a kitchen chair
b) a large dining table
c) a house

1 SLIME BONUS POINT

Answers on page 102

BODY QUIZ ANSWERS

Body Quiz 1

1) b   2) a   3) c   4) b   5) c   6) c   7) b   8) b   9) b   10) b

Body Quiz 2

1) b   2) c   3) b   4) a   5) c
6) a   7) a   8) a   9) b   10) a

Body Quiz 3

1) a   2) b   3) c   4) a   5) b
6) b   7) c   8) b   9) a   10) b

Body Quiz 4

1) b   2) c   3) a   4) c   5) c
6) a   7) a   8) c   9) c   10) b

Body Quiz 5

1) c   2) b   3) b   4) b   5) a
6) a   7) b   8) b   9) c   10) b

Incredibly Strange Science Facts

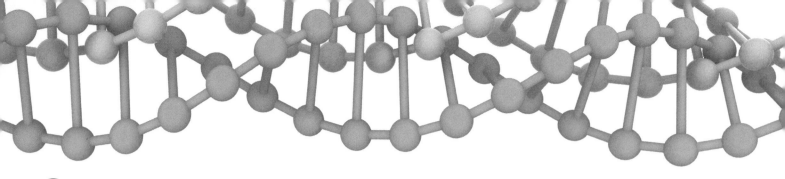

If a person is struck by lightning, they sometimes vaporize (evaporate) completely, so that there is nothing left of them at all.

Bacteria trapped inside a salt crystal for 250 million years were revived and grown by scientists in the USA.

An Anglo-American company will store samples of your disease-fighting white blood cells, so that more can be made if you get ill.

It takes less than 0.1 g (0.004 oz) of the poison that is found in parts of the pufferfish to kill an adult human. However, some people eat the fish regularly as they know which bits to remove first!

Dead bodies can remain perfectly intact after many years. This can happen when fat in the body turns into a type of soap that doesn't rot.

Some substances affect your urine – if you eat lots of rhubarb, your urine will be orange, and blackberries can make it go red!

Malaria is a tropical disease spread by mosquitoes. Since the Stone Age, malaria has been responsible for half of all human deaths from illness.

Medical researchers studied 46 professional sword swallowers and discovered that sore throats are common among them, especially when they are training ... how surprising!

Each person's tongue print is unique.

In ancient times, Indian doctors used live ants to "stitch" wounds together. The doctor would hold the edges together and get the ant to bite through the skin. The ant's head would then be snapped off leaving its jaws as the "stitch"!

You're more likely to get ill from kissing another person than a dog. Even though a dog's mouth has as many germs as a human's, not as many of them are harmful to us.

Eating asparagus produces a chemical that makes urine smell strongly, although not everyone can smell it. Lucky them!

A sneeze travels at 161 km (100 miles) per hour.

People can be born with ears growing from their necks or chests.

There are more bacteria in your mouth than there are people in the whole world!

More people are allergic to cows' milk than to any other food or drink.

Rubbing yourself with a garlic clove is supposed to keep mosquitoes away ... and vampires ... and probably other people, too!

Electrical activity is detectable in a human brain up to 37 hours after death, possibly caused by chemical reactions.

The spice nutmeg is harmless if eaten in moderation, but deadly poisonous if injected. Beware!

Your stomach lining replaces itself every three days.

A rare response to a virus that normally causes warts can also lead people to develop brown growths, which make them look as though they are covered with tree bark.

There have been many cases of people spontaneously bursting into flames and dying. Often, their whole body is burned away. No one knows exactly why this spontaneous human combustion happens. What a way to go!

Your skin is shed and regrown around every 27 days. Most people get through around 1,000 skins in a lifetime.

There is enough acid in the human digestive system to dissolve an iron nail completely.

A single human hair can support the weight of an apple.

You lose around two billion skin cells every day, which adds up to around 2 kg (4.5 lb) in a year.

Every day, you produce enough saliva in your mouth to fill five cups.

A chemical found in asparagus attracts fish. During the First World War, American soldiers were issued with asparagus so that if they were stranded near water they could eat the asparagus, urinate in the water, and catch some fish to eat!

If you rubbed garlic on the bottom of your foot, it would be absorbed through your skin and eventually your breath would smell of garlic!

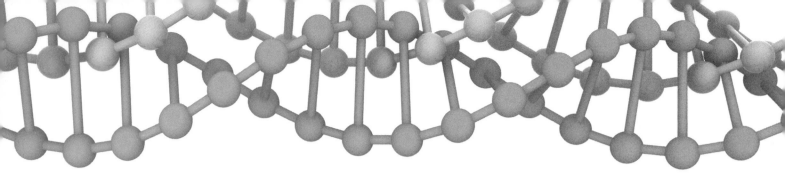

When you sneeze, all your bodily functions stop momentarily.

A traditional treatment for the pain of arthritis is bee venom … but then you're faced with the pain of bee stings!

If you have your head cut off, you may remain conscious and able to see for several seconds before you die.

About 125 g (5 oz) of the food you eat each day leaves the body as poop. Most of the rest is water, and the remainder consists of nutrients that are absorbed by your body.

In the 1930s, it was not uncommon for women to swallow live tapeworms in an attempt to lose weight. The tapeworms would live in their stomachs, eating some of the food the women ate.

Your fingernails grow four times faster than your toenails.

When you look at your tongue first thing in the morning, it is covered in white stuff. These are cells that died during the night.

Dripping concentrated oil from chillies into open wounds during surgery numbs the nerves for weeks and prevents patients feeling pain after an operation.

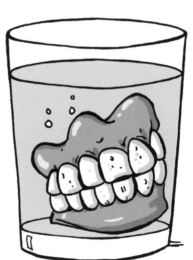

Forensic dentists examine teeth and tooth marks. Their work includes identifying dead bodies, and examining bite marks to match them to assailants.

Coffin flys are very small and so can find their way into coffins where they feed on corpses and lay their eggs.

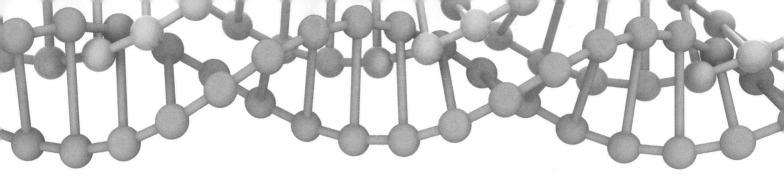

There are around 100 million microbes living in your mouth at any time. They feed on scraps of food and dead cells from your mouth.

The largest *coprolite* (fossilized dinosaur poop) measures 50 cm (19.6 in) and is from a Tyrannosaurus rex that lived more than 65 million years ago. It weighs around 7 kg (15 lb 6 oz).

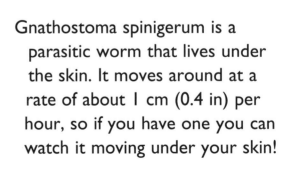

Doctors in the old days used leeches to extract people's blood. Today, doctors still use leeches in some surgical procedures, as they produce chemicals that kill pain and keep blood flowing without clotting.

Gnathostoma spinigerum is a parasitic worm that lives under the skin. It moves around at a rate of about 1 cm (0.4 in) per hour, so if you have one you can watch it moving under your skin!

The name for gurgling in the stomach is borborygmus.
It's caused by all the gases and half-digested food tumbling
around and being pushed through the gut.

Dandruff is made of clumps of dead skin cells mixed with
dirt and oil from your scalp. You lose millions of skin cells
each day, so there's plenty available to make dandruff!

There are 2,000 glands in your ear
that produce earwax. The sticky wax
collects dirt, dead bugs, and old skin
cells before it falls out of your ears.
It also kills germs!

The water in urine comes from your
blood. It goes from your food and drink
through the gut wall into the blood,
and is taken from the blood to
make urine.

Mucus in your nose collects all the dirt you breathe in, including particles of smoke, pollen, car fumes – and even dust from outer space! The slime and dirt clump together to make bogeys.

A pimple appears when a hair follicle becomes clogged by dried-up oil that oozes out of the skin.

Bile is the liquid that breaks down starches in your body. Bile from animals can be made into soap.

Sweat only smells bad because bacteria break it down when it stays on your skin. So, if your armpits or feet smell, it's rotting sweat helped along by colonies of bacteria.

The broad tapeworm can live in your gut for decades. You may not even know that you have one...

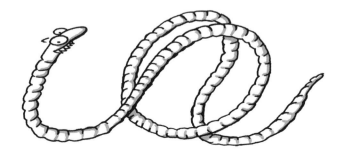

A porcupine can swallow 100 times the amount of poisonous hydrogen cyanide that is needed to kill a human and suffer no ill effects!

In the condition myiasis, maggots hatch out and live under the skin – they can even be seen wriggling around. In 1993, doctors in Boston, USA, developed a treatment for myiasis that involved covering the skin with bacon. Maggots like bacon, so move up toward it. Doctors then pull them out with tweezers. Gross!

Passing gas up to 21 times a day as burps and farts is quite normal. Nice!

Bacteria can survive 10,000 times the dose of radiation that would kill a person.

Tooth farming is an experimental technique in which scientists take dental stem cells (cells from immature teeth) and use them to grow complete teeth. So far, only parts of a tooth have been grown, but farmed teeth might replace dentures in 15 years' time.

Forensic scientists examine maggots and beetles eating dead bodies to try to work out the time that the person died. They study at which stages of decomposition the different bugs like to eat the body.

Your stomach uses hydrochloric acid to digest your food, but if you spill it on to your skin, it burns you. Your stomach produces mucus to protect itself from the acid. When someone dies and the mucus stops, the acid starts to dissolve the stomach.

Ancient Greek doctor Hippocrates used to diagnose people by tasting their blood, earwax, phlegm, and sometimes even urine!

Every drop of your saliva contains millions of bacteria, and not all of them have even been officially discovered yet!

There are several medical conditions that lead people to act like or believe they are wild animals such as wolves. These may explain some of the stories about werewolves.

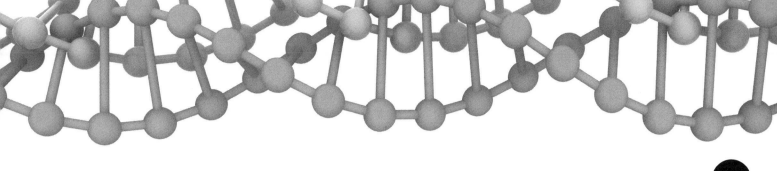

Roy Sullivan of the USA survived being struck by lightning seven times ... but eventually committed suicide.

Putrescine, one of the smelly chemicals produced by rotting dead bodies, is also partly responsible for bad breath.

A tsunami, a tidal wave often caused by an earthquake, can travel at up to 800 km (500 miles) per hour across open water.

Some people pay to have their bodies frozen after death in case scientists work out a way to bring them back in the future!

When people die in extreme circumstances their muscles can go into spasm and freeze in their final position. Forensic scientists can use this to show that someone was still alive when pushed into a river, for example, or died holding a weapon.

Fleas that live on rats spread bubonic plague, which killed around a third of the population of Europe in the 14th century. They only started to bite humans because all the rats died.

A cockerel that was inexpertly beheaded in 1945 lived for 18 months without its head! The farmer who owned the cockerel named him Mike, took him on tour, and earned a small fortune!

The placenta (the organ which grows to nourish a baby inside its mother) uses the same biological tricks as a parasitic worm to hide from the mother's immune system. Without it, the mother's body would reject the baby as an intruder.

A blackhead is black because the oily gunk in it changes to black on exposure to the air.

If a wound gets infected, find some maggots to put on it! They will eat all the rotten flesh and protect you from gangrene.

The nastiest form of the disease malaria can cause the
blood vessels in the brain to clog up with dead blood cells,
causing deadly spasms.

In the First World War, soldiers used the absorbent
sphagnum moss to bandage their wounds. It can soak up
four times as much blood as cotton bandages, but looked
disgusting – like dried pus!

Tenrecs (Madagascan hedgehogs) are so greedy they often
eat until they are sick.

Scientists have recreated the deadly flu
virus that killed one percent of the entire
world population between 1918 and 1919.
Smart, huh?

You will probably produce enough
saliva during your lifetime to fill two
swimming pools.

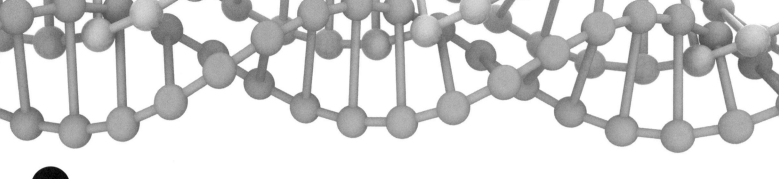

A virus can only survive in a host cell that is alive, so it's not in the interests of a virus to kill you. Even so, viruses caused all pandemic illnesses except bubonic plague, so don't get too relaxed about them!

Early anatomists were not allowed to study dead bodies, so they paid grave robbers to steal them. Often, the bodies of executed criminals were stolen and sold for this purpose.

A flea carrying bubonic plague gets blocked up with plague bacteria. When it bites its animal host, it vomits up the bacteria into the bite.

If you don't have enough water, eventually your lips shrivel and go black, your tongue swells so that it won't fit in your mouth, and you can go nearly deaf and blind, your breath stinks, your spit turns gluey and smelly, and if you cut yourself you don't bleed. So make sure you drink up!

The human stomach can hold up to 4 l (7 pt) of partly-digested food. A cow's stomach can hold ten times as much – enough to fill a whole bath!

Casper's Law of decomposition states that a body left in the open air decomposes twice as fast as if it were immersed in water and eight times faster than if it were buried underground.

Xenographic transplants involve taking an organ from an animal and using it in a human being – a chimpanzee heart was transplanted into a man in Mississippi, USA, in 1964, but the patient died two hours later.

Occasionally a baby is born with its legs fused together, but still with two feet. This mutation might have led to "true" stories of mermaids.

Rats can't vomit or belch. Rat poison kills them effectively because they can't throw it up once they've eaten it.

Stone Age people used trepanning – an early medical procedure that involved drilling a hole in the skull. They had no pain relief, so it must have hurt, but the patients didn't all die – lots of skulls have been found with partly healed holes!

Moths, butterflies, beetles, and mites eat the various algae that grow on a sloth.

A new way of treating cancer involves blowing bubbles inside the body. When the bubbles burst, they release heat, which kills the cancer cells.

It's possible that hiccups come from our very distant ancestors who crawled out of swamps and had both lungs and gills. Hiccups may be a remnant of a way they closed off their lungs when in water.

Your skin weighs about 3 kg (6.5 lb) – the same as a bag of potatoes.

People in some countries used to bind their babies' heads – sometimes to wooden boards – to make them grow into strange shapes … don't try it with your baby brother or sister!

A man born in England long ago was said to have had four eyes, positioned one pair above the other. He could close any one eye independently of the others.

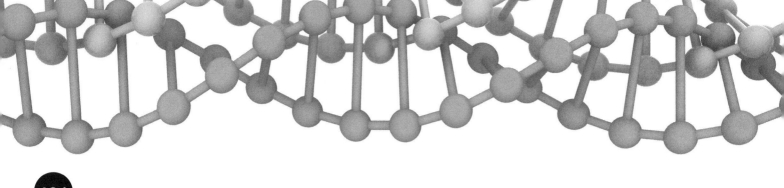

Washing towels and underwear together means that towels can become contaminated with poop.

Being born with webbed hands or feet is quite common. It happens because fingers and toes develop from an unborn baby's flipper-like hand or foot, which divides to form a proper hand or foot. If it doesn't divide properly, the skin stays webbed.

Some people have an abnormality called "hairy tongue" which gives them – you guessed it – a hairy tongue! In fact, it's not hair, but extra long *papillae* (the little bumps on your tongue). They also turn black!

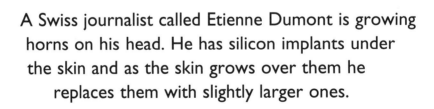

A Swiss journalist called Etienne Dumont is growing horns on his head. He has silicon implants under the skin and as the skin grows over them he replaces them with slightly larger ones.

Every year you eat about 500 kg (1,100 lb) of food. That's about the same weight as a small car!

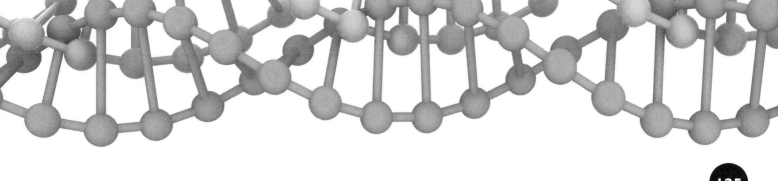

Items found inside the stomachs of sharks include a horse's head, a porcupine, parts of bicycles and cars, paintbrushes, a sheep, a chicken coop, and bottles of wine!

Ebola fever is a horrible disease that makes people bleed from all their body openings, and turns their internal organs to liquid. Victims always die.

A shark will carry on feeding even when another shark is eating it! It will also eat parts of its own body that have been bitten or cut off.

Many victims of the flu pandemic in 1918 went deep purple just before dying. Their lungs were so badly damaged by the disease that no oxygen could get into their blood.

You have more bacteria than human cells in your body.

Strychnine poisoning causes extreme muscle spasms. They can be so severe that the body can jerk backward until the heels touch the back of the head and the face is drawn into a terrifying, wide, fixed grin.

Some octopuses have been known to remove the stings from jellyfish they have caught and use them as weapons.

In 2002 German anatomist Gunther von Hagens carried out the first public autopsy for 170 years in London. However, it was illegal. The police attended, but did not stop the autopsy or arrest von Hagens, and the autopsy was even broadcast on television.

Having hookworms inside your body can protect you from asthma. Some people have deliberately infested themselves with hookworm to get rid of their asthma.

It is possible to die in just four minutes from choking or a blocked windpipe.

18th-century Italian scientist Lazzaro Spallanzani often made himself sick to get samples of stomach acid for his experiments.

The most dangerous animal to humans is the house fly – it carries more diseases than any other creature.

The human intestine is 9 m (nearly 30 ft) long. Just as well it's all coiled up!

In 1822 a man called Alexis St Martin was shot in the stomach. A doctor called William Beaumont cared for him, but the wound didn't heal completely and the man was left with a hole leading right into his stomach. Beaumont used it to study the workings of the stomach. St Martin's meals used to leak out of the hole unless he kept it covered!

When tree-living sloths descend once a week to go to the toilet, moths that live in their fur lay their eggs in the poop – the larvae can then enjoy a delicious meal when they hatch!

Some of the *Fore* people of New Guinea suffered from a strange illness that caused shaking, paralysis, and death; it puzzled doctors for years. It was eventually discovered that the disease, *kuru,* was caused by eating the undercooked brains of dead relatives, part of the Fore people's burial ritual.

Bodies buried in a peat bog may be naturally preserved for hundreds or even thousands of years. *Bog bodies* have dark leathery skin, but are still recognizable.

Hookworms enter through the feet, are carried in the blood to the lungs, and then travel up into the throat to be swallowed. The gut is their final destination – they bite onto it and live there.

In 1954 Russian scientist Vladimir Demikhov created a two-headed dog by grafting the head and front legs of a puppy onto a full-grown dog. The two heads would sometimes fight. The animal lived six days, but later he made one that lived a month. Freaky!

Bubonic plague has not disappeared from the world completely. An epidemic in Vietnam between 1965 and 1970 affected up to some 175,000 people.

Anatomist Gunther Von Hagens offered to buy the body of Russian basketball player Alexander Sizonenko, who was 2.39 m (7 ft 10 in) tall, even though he was still alive at the time! However, Sizonenko refused.

People with the condition Cotard syndrome believe that they are already dead, and are walking corpses.

American scientist Robert Cornish carried out an experiment to try to bring animals back from the dead by moving their bodies up and down on a seesaw to get their blood flowing again.

Some tortoises urinate on their back legs to keep themselves cool in the desert. The evaporating water takes away body heat. But they must smell a bit!

Owls eat small animals such as mice whole. They then vomit up the bones and fur in compact pellets.

In a rare mutation, chick embryos can grow teeth like crocodiles.

In 1846 two desert snails were given to a museum. Staff assumed they were dead and glued them to a display board. Four years later they noticed one was still alive! After removal of the glue and a warm bath, it recovered!

An octopus will eat itself if it becomes extremely stressed.

Moray eels have two sets of teeth in their throats. The first set of teeth bite onto an animal, then the second set move up into the eel's mouth, locking onto the prey. Finally, the first set of teeth move along the animal, dragging it into the eel's mouth.

The largest known spider was a goliath bird-eating spider found in Venezuela in 1965. It measured 28 cm (11 in) across!

In just ten years, a poisonous spider called the *false widow* has colonized southern England. It arrived in bunches of bananas, and warm weather has allowed it to survive. There are now tens of thousands running wild!

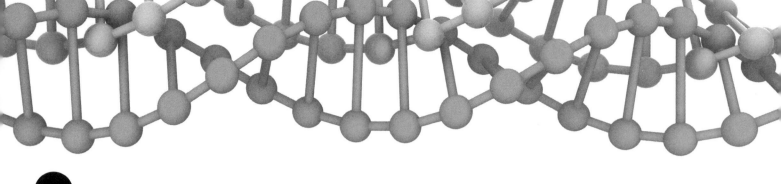

The curly heaps of earth you find on the ground are worm casts – which are made of worm poop.

A ribbon worm can eat 95 percent of its own body without dying. It only does this if there is nothing else to eat.

The vampire squid has eyes that make up an eleventh of its body length. It's as if a human had eyes the size of a table tennis bat!

The total weight of all the earthworms in the USA is about fifty times the total weight of all the human beings who live there.

The slime produced by snails is so protectively slimy that a snail could crawl along the edge of a razor blade without cutting itself.

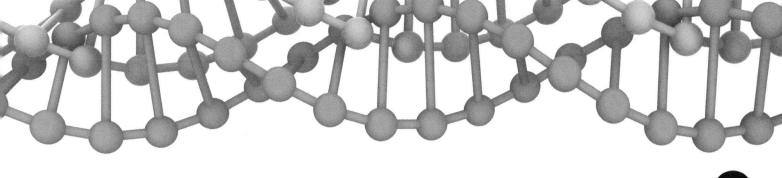

A rattlesnake's venom stays poisonous for up to 25 years after the rattlesnake has died.

Slugs have four noses.

Scientists sometimes pick apart owl pellets to find out what they've been feeding on. You can even buy owl pellets to examine at home – so get some owl vomit and try it yourself! Eugh!

Lobsters carry on shedding their shells as they grow, eating the shells they have outgrown.

An Asian salamander, frozen in ice in Siberia for 90 years, walked away after it was defrosted. The salamander usually lives for only 10 years, and hibernates during the winter, but this one got trapped under a frozen ice plug.

Queen termites lay an egg every second for up to 50 years.

Some types of baby spider in Australia bite the legs off their mother and eat them over several weeks.

The tarantula wasp will paralyze a tarantula spider and then lays its eggs in its live body. When the larvae hatch, they eat the spider alive!

Mosquitoes are attracted to humans by the smell of our feet more than any other part of the body.

Occasionally, snakes are born with two heads. When this happens, the heads often fight each other for food.

A cockroach can live for more than a week after its head has been cut off. Eventually, it starves to death.

When a frog is sick, it throws up its entire stomach, which then hangs out of its mouth. It uses its arms to scoop out the contents of the stomach and then swallows it again.

A leech doesn't need to eat often – cells from a meal enjoyed 18 months before can sometimes be found in its stomach.

There are 35,000 species of spider but only 27 are known to be able to kill humans.

Eighty percent of all living things are nematode worms – simple worms found everywhere including salt and fresh water, soil, and inside plants and animals.

In 1915 a terrible plague of locusts in Jerusalem darkened the sky in the middle of the day, blocking out the sun. They ate everything and laid millions of eggs. Even though all men between 15 and 60 years old had to collect 5 kg (11 lb) of eggs each to be destroyed, 99 percent of those laid still hatched.

A frog being sick was first observed when one was taken on a space flight.

White's tree frog is pale green in the sunlight but turns white when it goes into the shade. It lives in trees – and toilet cisterns! It's often found in toilets in Australia and New Guinea.

Roasted scorpions glow green under UV light.

Cockroaches have been around for at least 300 million years – that's 100 million years before the dinosaurs evolved.

The parasite, *toxoplasma,* prefers to live in cats' brains, but it can also infect rats, changing their brains so they are less scared of cats. This makes the rats more likely to be caught and eaten, allowing the parasite to move into the cat!

When they eat, planarian worms shoot a tube out of their throats to hold down their prey. They ooze enzymes out to soften the prey and then tear bits off it to eat.

There have been rainstorms with falling fish, frogs, and toads!

A giant squid washed up in Canada in 1878 had a body that was 6 m (20 ft) long with tentacles that measured up to 10.7 m (35 ft) long.

Newts can grow new body parts that have been lost or damaged, including legs, eyes, and even hearts. Scientists wonder if one day they might be able to persuade human bodies to do the same.

A bacterium in spoiled food, which causes the food poisoning botulism, is one of the deadliest known poisons – 450 g (1 lb) of the bacteria could wipe out the human race.

Stinging nettles grow well in soil that contains dead bodies – they thrive on a chemical called phosphorous which is in bones.

The bombadier beetle produces tiny explosions – up to 500 a second – which blast gases out of its rear end to frighten predators. The exploding farts sound like a machine gun!

In Australia in 2000, a plague of 100 billion locusts attacked wheat and barley crops.

Worms don't chew their food – they swallow small stones, which grind up the leaves and other vegetable matter they eat. Other animals also keep stones in their innards to break up their food – even the dinosaurs did it!

Planarians are a type of flatworm. They can regenerate (grow new body parts) even from a single, tiny piece of their body. A planarian can grow many heads and if it's cut up, the little bits make lots of new ones!

The taste of rat poison varies in different countries. It is adapted to suit the food rats are most used to.

A leech can suck five times its own body volume in blood at a single meal, in only 20 minutes.

The glass frog is lime green but has a completely transparent stomach. It's possible to see the blood vessels, the heart, and even check whether it's eaten recently or might like a snack.

Leafcutter ants mix chewed-up leaves with spit and droppings to make yummy compost. They also grow fungus on their compost heaps to eat.

The gulper eel lives in the deep sea, up to 5 km (3.1 miles) down and can grow to 2 m (6.6 ft) long. Its hinged mouth opens to more than 180 degrees, allowing it to swallow enormous prey even bigger than itself.

The darkling beetle lives in the desert where it's hard to find a drink. It sticks its front end into the sand and leaves its back end sticking up at night. Fog condenses on its behind, then runs down the beetle's body into its mouth. Ingenious!

Oysters can change sex several times during their lives.

Scientist Laurence M Klauber (1883–1968) was known as "Mr Rattlesnake" – he collected 35,000 pickled snakes and reptiles over his life to study.

The corpse flower or stinking lily is the smelliest flower in the world. Its stench is disgusting – it smells like a rotting corpse. This attracts insects that feed on the dead matter, and they pollinate the flower.

A type of carnivorous plant found in the tropical rainforests of Asia can "eat" birds and even rats. Animals are attracted by the nectar of the flower, and then fall into a vat of chemicals which dissolve them, feeding the plant.

In 1986, 92 people were killed in Bangladesh by hailstones that weighed over 1 kg (2.2 lb) each.

Getting parasites is a pain, but getting parasitoids means certain death – they live on or inside you, gradually eating you! But they mostly occur only in insects, so you don't need to worry (unless you're an insect).

Scientists working in the rainforests often find their feet go green and yucky with a fungus. It is usually found on old leaves on the forest floor, but is just as happy living on a wet, smelly foot.

A new species of the carnivorous pitcher plant was found in the Philippines in 2009, big enough to drown a rat.

The most poisonous plant in the world is the castor bean. Just 70 micrograms (2 millionths of an ounce) is enough to kill an adult human. It's 12,000 times more poisonous than rattlesnake venom.

The South American stinkhorn fungus smells of rotten meat and old toilets and has a slimy white spike which is irresistible to flies. Not a good houseplant for your bedroom!

A Venus flytrap is a carnivorous plant that traps and eats flies. It doesn't strike quickly – it takes half an hour to squash a fly and kill it, and another ten days to digest it.

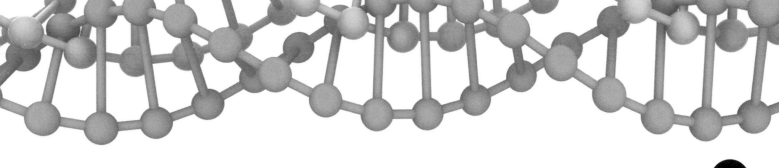

Cyanide is a poison that can be made from several plants.
A tiny amount is deadly in just five minutes.

Most bacteria are absolutely tiny – there can be as many as 50 million bacteria in a single drop of liquid.

Some plants, including grass, produce a poison when something starts to eat them. This is a chemical response to protect the rest of the plant.

A puffball fungus can release 7 billion spores in a single day. Luckily, they don't all grow, or there would be fungi everywhere you looked!

Some fungi glow in the dark and can be seen from 15 m (50 ft) away. They are used as natural lanterns.

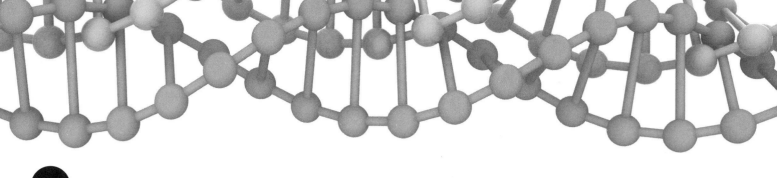

A pinch of soil holds 5 billion bacteria – nearly enough for everyone on the planet to have one each!

The durian fruit smells foul – like rotting fish – but tastes great! Orang-utans love it.

A tromatolite is a blob of algae and mud found on Australian beaches, naturally sculpted into the shape of a mushroom.

Instead of guard dogs, trumpet trees have "guard ants" living in their trunks! In return for their home, the Azteca ants bite anything that nibbles on the tree and then squirt acid into the creature's wound to make it extra sore. Ouch!

There are 1,500 types of insect in one rainforest tree in the Amazon, including 50 types of ant!

Plants often grow inside the skeletons of dead bodies in the Arctic – they make warm homes and have lots of nutrients that nourish plants.

The largest bacteria are 1 mm (0.039 in) long and are big enough to see with the naked eye.

Some explorers have drunk the juice inside pitcher plants – a mixture of the plant's acidic digestive juices and its half-dissolved victims. Yum.

The pink petticoat plant has a flower that looks like a pretty petticoat – it might look nice but it gobbles up bugs that crawl inside it.

The anacampseros plant looks like a bird dropping to protect it from being eaten by animals.

British scientists found that a robotic nose is better at detecting smells if it is given a coating of artificial bogeys!

When polar ice melts, it sometimes reveals mammoths frozen since the end of the last ice age. The mammoth meat can still be fresh – on one occasion, dogs ate the defrosted mammoth before scientists could investigate it!

Inside the vents of active volcanoes, bacteria live in conditions equivalent to a vat of hydrochloric acid. They're not fussy about their homes!

Amazonian Indians heat poison arrow frogs over a fire to sweat the poison out of them. They use the poison to tip their hunting arrows.

Earthrace is said to be the world's fastest eco-boat. It's partly powered by biofuel made from human fat from its crewmembers!

Some seeds eat meat! The seeds of shepherd's purse fill with water, swell up and burst – revealing a slimy layer. Bugs that stick to the slime are dissolved as the slimy seeds eat them

In the last 550 million years, there have been five events that have each destroyed at least 50 percent of all life on the planet.

The effects of global warming can be extreme – rising temperatures leading to catastrophic floods and droughts could destroy many plants animals and humans in years to come.

The lava (molten rock) that erupts out of a volcano can be as hot as 1,200 degrees Celsius (2,200 degrees Fahrenheit) and the power of a large eruption can equal that of a million nuclear bombs.

One of the largest volcanic eruptions recorded in recent history occurred on the island of Krakatau in Indonesia in 1883. It was so huge that most of the island disappeared into the sea!

Lake Nyos in Cameroon, Africa, belches out deadly carbon dioxide. Its poisonous burps killed 1,800 people in one night in August 1986. No one really knows where the gas comes from.

Increasing global temperatures could lead to an increase in diseases around the world – they will spread more easily and the weather won't be cold enough to kill them off.

Scorching hot winds from a volcanic eruption can travel at 300 km (185 miles) per hour, burning everything in their path at up to 800 degrees Celsius (1,470 degrees Fahrenheit).

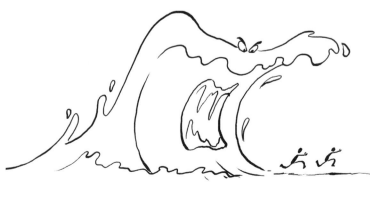

The tsunami in the Indian Ocean in 2004 killed around 230,000 people and was the ninth deadliest natural disaster since the Middle Ages.

When the Laki volcano in Iceland erupted in 1783, poisonous gas clouds swamped the land, killing half the country's livestock. A fifth of the human population starved to death.

You can die of thirst in the desert in only two days. You need to drink 9 l (about 16 pt) of water a day to stay healthy on a desert trek!

Mass extinctions of life on Earth appear to happen about every 26 million years. So don't worry just yet!

More people die in floods than in other type of natural disasters. The floods China in 1931 killed between one and four million people, and is the deadliest known natural disaster.

Bear poop is an essential part of the North American ecosystem! Grizzly bears eat salmon from the streams and then deposit vital nutrients on the land in the form of droppings and leftover fish.

Some astronauts have suffered from an illness called lunar lung caused by breathing in moon dust.

NASA – the National Aeronautics and Space Administration founded in the USA in 1958 – has developed ways to collect sweat from exercising astronauts to convert into drinking water for them in space. They can also do this with urine!

Astronauts wear special underpants during take off, landing and on space walks, as they can't go to the lavatory at these times!

If you went into a black hole, your body would be "spaghettified" – drawn out into an incredibly long, thin strand. Best not try!

The "Vomit Comet" is the name given to an aircraft that flies in such a way that it produces weightlessness. It's used to train astronauts, carry out research, and even make movies. It tends to make people sick, as you could probably guessed…

On the International Space Station, all waste from the lavatories is stored in a supply craft called *The Progress*. The craft is eventually released and burns away in Earth's atmosphere.

Astronaut sleeping bags are attached to the walls, floor, or ceiling so they don't float about while sleeping – there is no up or down is space.

Each astronaut has their own personal urine funnel, which they attach to the space station toilet.

Aconite is one of the most deadly poisons known – yet it is used in homeopathic remedies as a medicine!

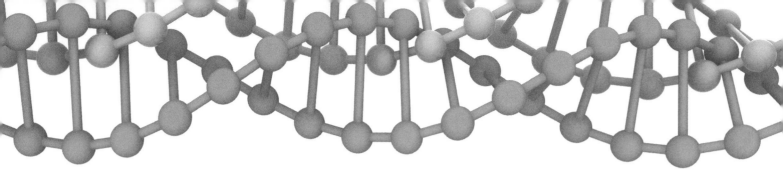

Doctors in ancient Egypt would give patients an electric shock with a catfish to treat the pain caused by arthritis.

Many types of toothpaste contain the skeletons of microscopic creatures from the sea, called diatoms.

Antifreeze is deadly poisonous – some governments insist that manufacturers add a chemical to make it taste horrible to stop people and animals from drinking it.

Human bodies decay more slowly than they used to as our food is now packed with preservatives that make their way into our bodies – and preserve us too!

The slime produced by a slug produces a small electric current when smeared over copper. Slug-powered mobile phone, anyone?

French scientist Antoine-Francois Fourcroy had the delightful job of studying the effects of heat, air, water, and other chemicals on rotting corpses.

Phosphorous (the chemical used for making matches) was first created when chemists extracted it from their urine. The urine was left to stand until it putrefied (went bad). It was later extracted from burned and crushed bones.

An American inventor has built a computer inside a stuffed, dead beaver.

People have known that the lead in paint is poisonous since at least 1904 – but lead paint was still widely used until the mid-1960s.

The water you get from the tap has been through many other people's bodies before it gets to you. But don't worry – it's been cleaned!

A traditional recipe for plant fertilizer consisted of rotten cow dung, ground up bones and, dry blood. These days you can buy a ready-made variety from the garden store.

The stuff that gives blue cheese its special smell and taste is related to penicillin, an antibiotic that you might be given when you're ill.

Arsenic was so commonly used as a poison by murderers in the 1800s, that in 1840 a law was passed in Britain saying that arsenic must be mixed with a blue or black dye so that people could see it in their food. It might have been better to stop pharmacists selling it…

Science Quiz 1

1 Why did women in the 1930s swallow wiggling tapeworms to live in their stomachs?

a) to cure stomach aches
b) to lose weight
c) to stop their farts smelling

2 The oil from which food is thought to numb intense pain after surgery?

a) chillies
b) almonds
c) cloves

3 What freaky super-animal have genetic scientists recently created?

a) a mighty mouse
b) a giant gerbil
c) a power pig

4 The dead horse arum plant's rotting smell lures which creatures to pollinate it?

a) frogs
b) horses
c) blowflies

REALLY HORRID!

5 Which hideous infection makes your body tissue decay and turn black?

a) gangrene
b) swine flu
c) malaria

1 SLIME BONUS POINT

6 What happens to a goldfish if you keep it in the dark?

a) it goes mad
b) it turns white
c) it grows fangs

7 Which country claims to have developed a dog food that reduces your pet's poop?

a) Singapore
b) Holland
c) USA

1 SLIME BONUS POINT

8 Roughly how many people does lightning kill each year?

a) 20
b) 200
c) 2,000

9 What temperature can the burning hot winds produced by a volcanic eruption reach?

a) 100°C(212°F)
b) 500°C (932°F)
c) 800°C (1,472°F)

10 What is the name of the horrible illness that some astronauts suffered after breathing in moon dust?

a) cosmic cough
b) lunar lung
c) solar sneezes

Answers on page 168

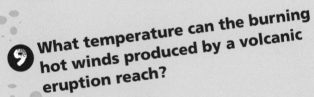

SCIENCE QUIZ 2

1 What may archeologists have discovered in an ancient Egyptian tomb?

   a) toenail cuttings
   b) nose hair
   c) pimple cream

REALLY HORRID!

2 What did World War I soldiers put on their wounds because it soaked up the blood?

   a) sphagnum moss
   b) cooked spaghetti
   c) squidgy horse poo

3 After hairy apes, what surprising animal is the closest relative to humans?

   a) a mouse
   b) a kangaroo
   c) a flying lemur

1 SLIME BONUS POINT

4 What do you call an infectious disease that spreads rapidly around the world?

   a) a pandemic
   b) an academic
   c) a medic

5 How much faster do your fingernails grow than your toenails?

   a) twice as fast
   b) four times as fast
   c) eight times as fast

6 What is the name given to a research establishment where decomposing bodies are studied?

a) a rot farm
b) a corpse farm
c) a body farm

7 What did early surgeons test out their knife skills on?

a) dead farm animals
b) stolen corpses
c) their fellow surgeons

8 Which fruit smells of rotten fish but tastes great?

a) a prickly pear
b) a dragon fruit
c) a durian fruit

1 SLIME BONUS POINT

9 Which scientist created yucky germ paintings using living bacteria?

a) Charles Darwin
b) Alexander Fleming
c) Albert Einstein

10 What hideous thing happened to Laika, the first dog to travel into space?

a) she overheated and died
b) her brains exploded
c) she got stuck in a moon crater

Answers on page 168

SCienCe QUiZ 3

1 Roughly how long does it take for a banana to decompose?

a) four days
b) four weeks
c) four months

2 Roughly how many seeds of the deadly raw castor bean do you need to eat for it to kill you?

a) 1
b) 8
c) 18

3 What is a more common name for mycetism?

a) migraine
b) mumps
c) mushroom poisoning

REALLY HORRID!

4 Blood-sucking mosquitoes are attracted to people who eat which fruit?

a) oranges
b) pineapples
c) bananas

1 SLIME BONUS POINT

5 Which greedy animals devour 10 percent of the world's food supply?

a) insects
b) fish
c) reptiles

6 **What is *botulism*?**

a) a spotty bottom
b) a type of food poisoning
c) a scabby skin disease

7 **How big is the atomic clock, developed in the USA that will keep time forever?**

a) the size of a grain of rice
b) the size of a tennis ball
c) the size of a swimming pool

1 SLIME BONUS POINT

8 **Fierce whirlwinds over lakes can make twisting columns of water. What are they called?**

a) water devils
b) water monsters
c) water pipes

9 **What was once found inside a giant hailstone that fell to Earth?**

a) a frozen poop
b) a frozen turtle
c) a frozen skateboard

10 **Why might doctors cover a person's infected skin with strips of bacon?**

a) to remove maggots
b) to remove warts
c) to remove sores

Answers on page 168.

Science Quiz 4

1 How many electrifying bolts of lightning are striking Earth at any one time?

a) about 10
b) about 100
c) about 1,000

2 In which national park is there a super-volcano that could wipe out the USA?

a) Grand Canyon
b) Yosemite
c) Yellowstone

3 What causes a dead body to swell up as it rots?

a) maggot infestation
b) a build-up of gas
c) soil gets inside it

REALLY HORRID!

4 What is the medical condition *myiasis*?

a) maggots under your skin
b) fungus on your scalp
c) a runny bottom

5 What is the hugely whiffy *titan arum* plant also known as?

a) the poop plant
b) the corpse flower
c) the vomit spike

6 People scrub dead skin off their feet with pumice. What is it made from?

a) volcanic rock
b) household bricks
c) dried seaweed

7 Carnivorous plants usually munch insects but what else have they been known to eat?

a) hedgehogs
b) human toes
c) rats

8 How long does it take for a killer avalanche to reach its top speed?

a) five seconds
b) five minutes
c) five hours

1 SLIME BONUS POINT

9 In which of these places would you be guaranteed to freeze to death quickly outside?

a) Vostok Station
b) Chalk Farm Station
c) Grand Central Station

10 What are there three of on the moon?

a) burger wrappers
b) golf balls
c) human poop

Answers on page 168

Science Quiz 5

1 Which tree oozes a yucky red sap that looks like thick blood when it is cut?

   a) a redwood

   b) a bloodwood

   c) a maple

2 Which of these plants gobbles up unfortunate flies that crawl inside it?

   a) a pink petticoat

   b) a granny's bonnet

   c) an angel's trumpet

3 What do the slimy seeds of the shepherd's purse plant do after they have burst open?

   a) dry up

   b) munch mushrooms

   c) eat bugs

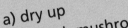

1 SLIME BONUS POINT

4 What might a dead body alarmingly do?

   a) fart

   b) cough

   c) talk

5 What lives in the vents of active volcanoes in a vat of acid?

   a) tubeworms

   b) yeti crabs

   c) bacteria

6 What would a human poop do in space?

a) float off and break up
b) evaporate into a stinky gas
c) turn black and rock hard

7 On rare occasions a snake might be born with two heads. What do the heads often do?

a) fight over food
b) one eats the other
c) kiss each other

8 What happened to one frozen mammoth in the Arctic after scientists discovered it?

a) it exploded
b) dogs ate it
c) it woke up

1 SLIME BONUS POINT

9 What is the largest living thing on planet Earth?

a) a blue whale
b) an enormous fungus
c) a giant tubeworm

10 The fruit of the *strychnine* plant looks like tiny oranges but what can it do to you?

a) poison you
b) rot your feet
c) blind you

Answers on page 168

SCIENCE QUIZ 6

1 What type of creature living in warm waters might swim up your nose and eat your brain?

a) a spider
b) a worm
c) an amoeba

2 In what bizarre vehicle did Marek Turowski reach a speed of 148 kmph/92 mph?

a) a motorized sofa
b) a jet-propelled plastic pig
c) a 30-wheeled bicycle

3 What cruel thing can happen to you before you die from mushroom poisoning?

a) you will go mad
b) your brain will dissolve
c) you will feel better

4 Up to how many beady eyes does a scallop have around its crusty shell?

a) 10
b) 100
c) 1,000

1 SLIME BONUS POINT

5 What is the name of the mental condition where a person thinks they are a wolf?

a) wolf syndrome
b) lycanthropy
c) shapeshifting

6 Our moon looks round, but what shape are the moons around Mars?

a) sausage-shaped like dog poop
b) thin and long like bananas
c) oval and bumpy like potatos

7 What can make a rubber band last longer?

a) rubbing it with spit
b) storing it in a tin
c) keeping it in the refrigerator

8 How much did the heaviest human brain ever recorded weigh?

a) 1.1 kg (2 lb 8.6 oz)
b) 2.3 kg (5 lb 1.1 oz)
c) 3.3 kg (7 lb 2.7 oz)

10 What powers the International Space Station?

a) solar panels
b) human toilet waste
c) giant batteries

9 What is a volcanic bomb?

a) another name for a nuclear explosion
b) a large rock spewed out of a volcano
c) a noisy exploding fart

Answers on page 168

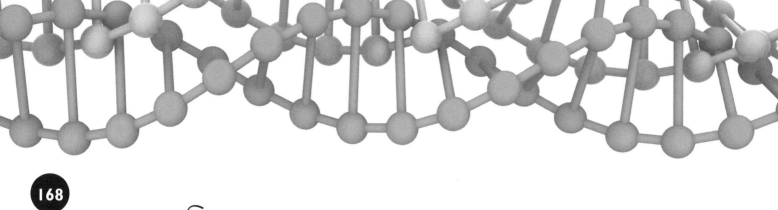

SCIENCE QUIZ ANSWERS

Science Quiz 1

1) b   2) a   3) a   4) c   5) a   6) b   7) b   8) c   9) c   10) b

Science Quiz 2

1) c   2) a   3) c   4) a   5) b   6) c   7) b   8) c   9) b   10) a

Science Quiz 3

1) b   2) b   3) c   4) c   5) a   6) b   7) a   8) a   9) b   10) a

Science Quiz 4

1) b   2) c   3) b   4) a   5) b
6) a   7) c   8) a   9) a   10) b

Science Quiz 5

1) b   2) a   3) c   4) a   5) c
6) a   7) a   8) b   9) b   10) a

Science Quiz 6

1) c   2) a   3) c   4) b   5) b
6) c   7) c   8) b   9) b   10) a

Incredibly Strange History Facts

Archeologists study coprolites (fossilized poop) to find out what people, animals, and even dinosaurs used to eat. Coprolites can even reveal any worms or parasites that people were infected with in the Stone Age.

Mammoths had a large, hairy flap of skin that covered their bottom to keep them warm!

The world's oldest building is a primitive shelter built in Japan around 498,000BC. It was discovered in the year 2000 – it must have been a bit smelly by then!

By 20,000BC people had worked out that an easy way to get lots of food at once was to drive a herd of animals over a cliff to kill them in one go. Remains of 100,000 horses have been found at the bottom of a cliff in France. That was probably more than they could eat in one sitting!

The paint used to make cave paintings was made from blood or animal fat mixed with mineral or plant pigments.

People living in Jericho in 7500BC took ancestor worship to the extreme! They'd remove the head of a dead grandparent, fill it with clay, paint the skull to look like flesh, and place shells in the eye sockets for eyes.

In Jericho around 7,000 years ago, people buried their dead under the dirt floor of their houses.

Woodhenge in Wiltshire, England, was originally a circle of wooden posts built around 4000BC. It's believed to have been a sacrificial site as bodies have been discovered, buried in the middle of the site.

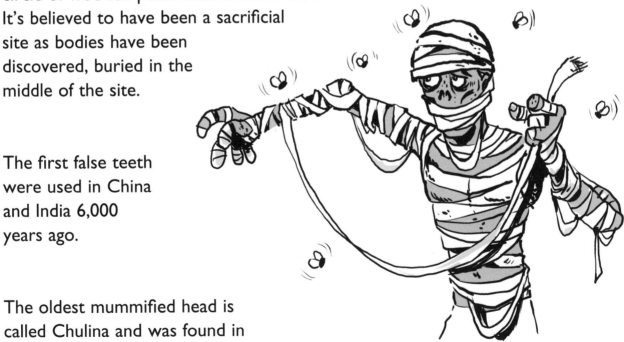

The first false teeth were used in China and India 6,000 years ago.

The oldest mummified head is called Chulina and was found in the Andes in South America.

Ancient Egyptians believed that if their body was left to rot, they wouldn't be able to reach the afterlife.

The earliest known murder victim was a man who had lived in the Italian Alps around 3300BC. His body, found in 1991, was preserved in ice with an arrowhead in his back.

When dead pharaohs were embalmed in ancient Egypt, the brain was hooked out through the nose or scooped out through an eye socket. Often, the brain was chopped up inside the skull with a wire first, to make it easier to get it out.

A French cure for headaches around 4000BC was to drill a hole in the patient's skull with a sharp stone to let out any evil spirits.

The ancient Egyptians had dental drills and were able to drill out decayed parts of teeth, but they are not known to have had any way to numb the mouth first. Ouch!

A pit containing the bones of animals eaten in prehistoric Russia also contained human bones, leading archeologists to think early people in the area were cannibals.

In Egypt the final stage of embalming a body was to place a golden "death mask" over the mummy's face, so that when the pharaoh's spirit returned to the tomb, he would recognize his body.

The ancient Assyrians had a habit of flaying (skinning) their enemies alive and hanging up their skins outside the city wall.

People in Mesopotamia believed in demons called *lilu* who were the spirits of people who had died unmarried. They came into homes looking for victims to marry them in the demon world.

Hundreds of bodies are burried under Stonehenge (a prehistoric monument in Wiltshire, England) but they aren't thought to have been human sacrifices. It's believed the site was used as a cemetery before the stones were put up.

Many mummies had black shiny stones put in their eye sockets, but pharoah Rameses IV had small onions instead!

Pharaoh Hor-Aha who reigned around 3050BC, was killed by a hippopotamus while he was on a hunting expedition.

Babylonian king Hammurabi was tough on unreliable builders. If a house collapsed due to poor workmanship and killed the owner, the builder was executed.

One way that archeologists find out what people ate in ancient times is by examining food found in the stomachs of mummified remains.

The first drunk driving conviction occurred in around 2800BC. A drunk Egyptian charioteer was arrested after running over a priestess. He was nailed to the door of a tavern and his corpse remained hanging there as a warning to others.

When a pharaoh died, Egyptians believed that his heart was weighed against a feather representing truth and justice. If the two sides of the scales balanced, he could enter paradise. Otherwise a monster would eat his soul and he'd be lost forever. Sounds fair...

Before embalming the body, a pharaoh's vital organs (the lungs, liver, stomach, and intestines) were removed and stored in special jars to be placed in his tomb.

Mummies were entombed with their mouths open so they could eat in the afterlife.

If a peasant didn't work hard enough in ancient Egypt, he would be whipped or have a toe or finger cut off.

Queen Puabi of Mesopotamia died around 2600BC. Her grave contains the bodies of 5 armed guards and 23 ladies in waiting. The lucky servants were poisoned so they could accompany their queen to the next world.

In the "opening of the mouth" ceremony, an ancient Egyptian priest would touch a mummy's mouth with a blade, rub its face with milk, and hug the bandaged corpse. People believed the dead man could then eat, drink, and move!

An ancient Egyptian cure for blindness was the mashed eyeball of a pig, mixed with honey and red earth, poured into the ear.

Ancient Egyptians used a naturally occurring soap-like substance called natron to wash themselves in the bath. They used the same substance when mummifying dead people – so it was best not to lie too still in the bath in case someone got confused!

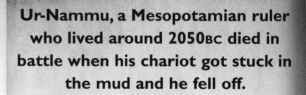

Ur-Nammu, a Mesopotamian ruler who lived around 2050BC died in battle when his chariot got stuck in the mud and he fell off.

In 1750BC the Babylonian king Hammurabi established a particularly harsh set of laws. Punishments included cutting off a finger or hand for theft and cutting off a man's lower lip for kissing a married woman.

When a king died in ancient China, thousands of slaves and prisoners of war could be sacrificed as a display of respect and an offering to their god.

Careless embalmers accidentally wrapped flies, lizards, and even a mouse into some mummies' bandages!

In 1580BC pharoah Apophis of Upper Egypt sent this message to pharoah Sekenenre of Lower Egypt: "The farting of the hippopotami swimming in the temple pool at your palace is keeping me awake. Do something about it or else!" Apophis' palace was over 640 km (397 miles) away, so Sekenenre took this as an insult and immediately declared war.

It is thought that pharaoh Seqenenre, who reigned around 1550BC, was killed in battle. His mummified corpse has head wounds from a spear, a club, and a dagger. There's nothing like making sure…

The ancient Egyptians believed that onions would keep bad spirits away. Friends and family too, perhaps!

After removing the innards and stuffing the body with natron, a mummy-to-be was left to dry out for 70 days before being wrapped. It was then stuffed with linen and straw to keep its shape – the pharaoh wouldn't want to turn up in the afterlife looking all saggy!

"Oracle bones" were used in ancient China to predict the future. They were made from pieces of animal bone or shell, or sometimes human bones.

Stone Age Australian men often had their two front teeth removed to show they were tough and manly.

The earliest death sentence is recorded on an ancient Egyptian scroll from about 1500BC. A teenage male, convicted of "magic" was sentenced to kill himself either by poison or stabbing. Executioners were a bit lazy back then.

Ancient Egyptian women put a cone of perfumed fat on their heads. As it melted in the heat, it made their hair smell nice. It can't have looked very good though!

The first instance of biological warfare may have been a terrible plague that struck the Hittites (an ancient Syrian civilization) in 1335BC. It's thought that the Hittites' enemies introduced tularemia (a deadly animal disease) by sending them infected rams.

Some Egyptian mummies show evidence of tapeworms being present. The tapeworms were not mummified separately!

Remains found in a mass grave in Dakota, USA, show that prehistoric warriors scalped their victims, probably to keep the hair as a trophy.

According to Babylonian king Hammurabi's law, if you stole from a burning house you would be burned alive, and charging too much for a drink was punishable by drowning!

When pharaoh Rameses II was mummified in 1212BC, the embalmers tried to keep his nose in shape by stuffing it with peppercorns!

Pharaoh Pepy II of Egypt always kept several naked slaves close by whose bodies were smeared with honey. This encouraged flies to land on them instead of on him! A very sticky business...

When the Nile failed to flood in the period 1073–1064BC, there was a great famine in Egypt and people resorted to eating each other.

Ancient Egyptians treated some infections with old, mildewy bread. As it happens, the fungus on old bread contains antibiotics, so it probably worked well.

The philosopher Heraclitus (535–475BC) tried to cure himself of dropsy (a disease which causes water on the lungs) by burying himself in a pile of cow dung. It didn't work. He just died smelly.

A well preserved bog man with six fingers was discovered in England. The man had been killed as a sacrifice in early Roman times.

Draco "the lawgiver" was the first person to establish law in Athens in 621bc. The punishment for any crime at all was death. Very severe laws are now said to be draconian.

During the siege of Megara, Greece, the Megarians poured oil over a herd of pigs, set fire to them, then drove the pigs at the war elephants of their enemies. The elephants bolted in terror from the squealing pigs and trampled the enemy soldiers.

Ancient Romans spread pigeon droppings on their hair to lighten it – the ammonia acted as a bleach. Hairdresser wouldn't have been a great job in those days...

Ancient Greeks didn't use napkins. Instead they wiped their hands on pieces of bread, then fed the bread to the dogs.

Despite his harsh laws, Draco of Athens was very popular. Legend has it that attending a reception one day, he was showered with hats, shirts, and cloaks by admiring citizens. By the time they dug him out from under the clothing he had suffocated to death.

Roman doctors had no way of offering their patients pain relief when they fixed broken bones or cut off rancid arms and legs. Instead, they were trained not to take any notice of the screams!

Alcmaeon of Croton, Greece, is the first person known to have studied the human body by cutting up corpses, around 520BC.

The Celts, who lived in Britain around 500BC, collected the heads of the people they slaughtered in battle. They stuck them on poles, threw them in rivers as gifts to the gods, nailed them to the walls as decorations, or hollowed them out to use as cups.

It's thought that Greek mathematician Pythagoras was beaten to death by an angry mob around 500BC. He could have run away, but he would have had to trample through a field of beans. Pythagoras believed that beans held the souls of dead ancestors, so he chose to die.

Ancient Romans believed the souls of the dead needed the odd human sacrifice. When someone died, it was the custom to spill human blood over their grave or tomb. Lazy slaves were often chosen as a sacrifice.

The first ever "marathon" was run by a Greek messenger called Pheidippides in 490BC. He ran 42 km (26 miles) from a town called Marathon to Athens to announce that the Greeks had beaten the Persians in a battle. As soon as he got there, he collapsed and died from exhaustion.

Spartans held whipping competitions. Whoever could stand the most whipping without making a fuss would win. You could even win if you died, but it wasn't as much fun.

To clean themselves, Romans poured olive oil all over their bodies then scraped off the oily, dirty gunk with a curved blade called a *strigil*. Yuk.

A terrible plague killed a third of the population of Athens in 430BC. Victims had a fever, headaches, stomach pain, and vomiting, and were covered in painful blisters. Those that didn't die often lost fingers, toes, or their sight. Historians still don't know what the disease was.

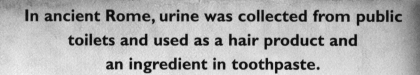

In ancient Rome, urine was collected from public toilets and used as a hair product and an ingredient in toothpaste.

When the Egyptian general Phanes swapped sides in a war and joined the enemy Persians, the angry Egyptians killed his sons and drank their blood.

In Kazakhstan around 300BC, a woman had her left foot amputated and replaced with two bones taken from a ram – the first attempt at a limb transplant.

The Chinese emperor Qin (259–210BC) was ruthless. Anyone who disobeyed him or argued against his rules was set to work building the Great Wall of China or buried alive.

The Chinese lord Shang (died 338BC) ordered everyone in the country to spy on each other. People were divided into groups of five or ten and had to report any offences. If they failed to report a crime, they were cut in half.

The punishment for killing a close relative in ancient Rome was to be sewn into a sack with a dog, a snake, a cockerel, and a monkey and thrown into the river Tiber.

The ancient Greek mathematician Archimedes used mirrors to focus sunlight on enemy ships so that they burst into flames.

A Greek cure for bad breath was to boil the head of a hare together with three mice and rub the resulting mixture on your gums. It probably covered up the original smell, but it wasn't necessarily any better!

In 212BC officers of the Chinese chancellor Li Si collected 460 of the country's greatest scholars and had them all buried alive in a mass grave. It wasn't a good time to admit to being really clever!

Both the Greeks and Romans believed they could tell the future by examining the pattern made by the guts spilled from a sacrificed bird. The future always looked grim for birds…

Spartacus led a lot of revolting slaves (slaves who were rebelling, not slaves who didn't wash) against the Romans who owned them. He died in battle, but 6,600 of his followers were crucified in rows lining the Appian Way, a highway that led to Rome.

King Mithridates VI of Pontus took small doses of poison throughout his life to build up his resistance in case someone tried to poison him. His plan backfired when he was captured by the Romans in 63BC. He tried to kill himself using poison but it had no effect! Instead he got a slave to kill him with a sword.

Gladiatorial games were first held at funerals. The Romans believed that spilling blood on their grave would help the dead person get to heaven.

A Roman remedy for baldness was a mixture of pigeon droppings, cumin, horseradish, and stinging nettles. Ouch!

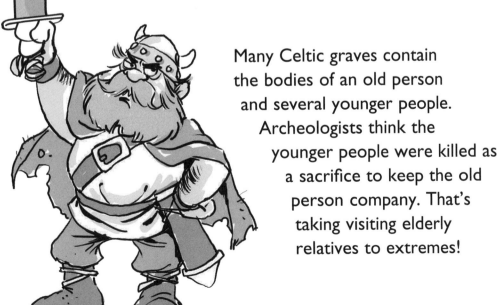

Many Celtic graves contain the bodies of an old person and several younger people. Archeologists think the younger people were killed as a sacrifice to keep the old person company. That's taking visiting elderly relatives to extremes!

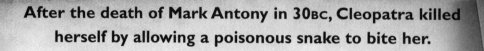

After the death of Mark Antony in 30BC, Cleopatra killed herself by allowing a poisonous snake to bite her.

Scythian soldiers had to collect the scalps of the people they killed. The scalps were a form of receipt – in exchange for each one they would win a share of the loot after a battle. A soldier with enough scalps could even make a nice cloak from them – very snug!

Wounded Roman soldiers used spiders' webs to help stick their wounds together. They also tucked herbs into their bandages to kill any germs.

The people of Thassos, Greece, built a statue of a famous boxer in the 5th century BC. A jealous opponent attacked the statue, which fell on him and squashed him. The statue was found guilty of murder and thrown into the ocean!

New Scythian soldiers had to drink the blood of the first enemy soldier they killed.

Criminals in Britain in the 5th century BC were thrown (alive) into a swamp known as a quagmire to drown.

Philoxenus of Leucas was a legendary glutton of the late 4th century BC. He spent hours hardening his fingers in hot water so he could grab the tastiest hot food from the table before anyone else.

In the 4th century BC, Spartan men were required by law to eat 1 kg (about 2 lb) of meat per day to make them braver.

The Roman ceremony of Lupercalia was celebrated in February. It involved killing two goats and a dog, and smearing blood from the goats on the foreheads of two young men. Then they had a feast, dressed up in the skins of the dead goats, and went around whipping people. They really knew how to party…

Wealthy Roman, Marcus Licinius Crassus, was killed by his enemies who poured molten gold down his throat.

Vedius Pollio, a rich Roman of the 1st century BC, kept a fish farm at his house where his pet fish were fed the bodies of dead slaves. It's said that he fed badly behaved slaves to his eels.

Human bodies dumped into bogs are sometimes preserved naturally for thousands of years. When workmen in Cheshire, England, dug up the body of a man, they called the police immediately. It turned out the murder had taken place 2000 years ago! He had been sacrificed by the Romans who had smashed his skull into his brain, slit his throat, and strangled him.

In Slovakia, in the 1st century BC, 12 people were beaten to death and cut into quarters. Their body parts were then dumped in a pit at a holy site, possibly to ensure a good harvest.

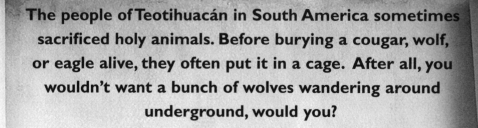

The people of Teotihuacán in South America sometimes sacrificed holy animals. Before burying a cougar, wolf, or eagle alive, they often put it in a cage. After all, you wouldn't want a bunch of wolves wandering around underground, would you?

The Huns, who lived in an area stretching from Germany to Russia, scarred their teenage sons' faces to make them look fiercer when they went into battle.

In Carthage in the 5th century AD, Christian women were catapulted into the air. The crash-landing was their punishment for deciding to be Christians.

In AD37 Roman emperor Caligula became seriously ill and went mad. He executed his loyal followers, banished his wife from Rome, and forced his father-in-law and cousin to commit suicide.

Honey-roasted dormouse was a delicacy in ancient Rome. Cooks kept the mice in terracotta jars and fattened them up for a few weeks first to make sure they were extra meaty.

To ensure her son Nero became emperor, Agrippina murdered her husband, emperor Claudius, with a plate of poisoned mushrooms in AD54.

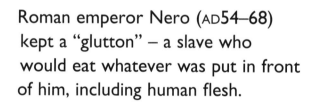

When the Romans conquered a country, they made all its young men join their army. Many didn't want to, so the Romans ruled that anyone who didn't fight would be executed.

Roman emperor Nero (AD54–68) kept a "glutton" – a slave who would eat whatever was put in front of him, including human flesh.

Spartan babies had to look tough from the moment they were born. Any baby that looked a bit weak was either abandoned on a hillside to die or thrown off a cliff.

The Huns placed slices of raw meat under their saddles so that it was tenderized as they rode their horses.

The Roman emperor Nero was guilty of many atrocities, even killing his own mother. He made sure the ship she was on sank, then when she swam to safety, he sent soldiers to kill her. All that after she'd poisoned her husband for him – how ungrateful!

In AD72 the Romans laid siege to a town in Palestine. When they finally broke through the town walls a year later, the Romans discovered that the 936 inhabitants had all killed themselves.

When the volcano Vesuvius erupted in AD79, thousands of people living in the towns of Pompei and Herculaneum were killed. They were scorched by burning winds, crushed under heaps of falling rubble, or killed by the fires that swept through the towns.

A scary lightning strike in AD228 led the Romans to bury two Greeks and two Celts under the Forum (the place in Rome where people met and business was conducted) while they were still alive. It was supposed to stop the gods being angry and sending more lightning.

St Ignatius was ripped apart by wild lions as punishment for being a Christian. He was taken from Turkey to Rome around AD100 and then thrown to the lions in the arena.

St Lawrence, an early Christian, was martyred in AD258 by being roasted on a fire. It's said that after a while he called out: "I am already roasted on one side and, if thou wouldst have me well cooked, it is time to turn me on the other."

The Roman emperor Elagabalus (AD218–222) was so extravagant that he once suffocated some dinner guests to death beneath a mass of sweet-smelling rose petals that he had dropped from the ceiling.

The female scholar Hypatia was murdered in AD415 by a group of crazed monks, who sliced her body into pieces with oyster shells.

One complicated Roman dish involved stuffing a chicken inside a duck, the duck inside a goose, the goose inside a pig, the pig inside a cow, then cooking the whole thing together!

It is said that Attila the Hun (who ruled the Hun kingdom between AD434–453) enjoyed the taste of raw flesh and human blood. It saved on cooking!

It was the custom in ancient Rome for men to place their right hand on their testicles when taking an oath. The modern term "testimony" is derived from this tradition.

Attila the Hun murdered his wife's brothers. In revenge, she served him the hearts of his two sons (Erp and Eitil) for dinner. What a nice couple...

Bald Romans made a paste from mashed up flies and spread it over their heads to encourage hair growth.

The Romans used to fatten snails to eat. They fed them first on salted milk and then plain milk, until they were so bloated that they couldn't fit back inside their shells. They were then fried and served with a wine sauce.

The fearless warrior Attila the Hun died in AD453, after getting a nosebleed on his wedding night with his new bride.

According to legend, when St Alban was beheaded around AD304, the executioner's eyes fell out.

In AD395 it was reported that the British Attacotti tribe were all cannibals who ate the fleshy parts of shepherds and their wives.

The Romans would use convicted criminals as actors in their more gory plays, so they could be tortured and provide entertainment at the same time. At the end of one play, the criminal had to be torn apart by a bear!

If a woman watched even one Olympic event in ancient Greece, she could be executed.

If a Roman owed a lot of people money, they were all allowed to take a sharp knife and cut a slice off him.

According to the Roman writer Tacitus, 50,000 people were killed when a badly built arena collapsed during a show. The screams of the injured people buried under the rubble could be heard all day and night.

A Roman cure for feeling unwell was to eat cabbage for a day, then drink the urine you produced. It probably made you forget the original illness!

When a holy person died in the Middle Ages, there would often be a frantic scramble to get a piece of the body – a toe, finger, or bone. People kept these parts, called *relics*, as they believed they had special powers, like being able to heal illness and protect people from evil.

In AD493 Theodoric, ruler of the German Ostrogoth tribe, defeated Odoacer, king of Italy, in battle. After making a toast at a feast celebrating their peace, Theodoric stabbed Odoacer to death.

The Saxons (a group of Germanic tribes who lived in Europe) had a unique cure for madness – make a whip from the skin of a dolphin, then beat yourself with it. You'd have to be mad to do something as strange as that!

In the Middle Ages, people cleaned the leg bones of sheep or pigs, then strapped them to their feet to use as ice skates!

Sometimes Saxon wives were buried alive with their husbands to keep them company in the afterlife. They must have made rather grumpy companions after being buried alive...

In 1016, King Edmund II of England was using the toilet when he was murdered. An assassin (who had hidden underneath) reached up and stabbed him in the bottom with a long knife. What a dirty job…

Mean Englishman John Overs pretended to die, expecting his servants to fast in mourning for him – saving him the cost of feeding them for a day. Instead, they had a party! When he shouted at them, the servants thought he was a ghost and battered him to death with an oar!

In about 1044, the Chinese invented the excrement bomb. The bomb was made from a mixture of human poop, gunpowder, and a few nasty chemicals!

In 1014 Byzantine emperor Basil II captured 15,000 Bulgarian prisoners of war. He blinded 99 out of every 100, and gouged out one eye from all the rest. This allowed the ones with a remaining eye to lead the others home. The Bulgarian ruler Samuel died instantly when he saw his blinded army.

Harold I of England made it a crime for any Welshman to carry a weapon. An armed Welshman would have his hand cut off … which instantly made him an unarmed Welshman!

In the Middle Ages, left-handed people were thought to be descended from the devil and were banned from becoming knights.

Becoming king turned out to be not so great for England's Harold I – he was crowned in 1066 and killed by William the Conqueror that same year.

When William the Conqueror attacked the city of Alençon, France, the people jeered at him. After he won the battle, he cut the hands and feet off 32 of the most noble citizens in revenge.

Hereward the Wake, a warrior who fought against the Normans in England, returned from battle to find his brother's head nailed over the door to his house. That night, Hereward cut the heads off 14 Norman soldiers and nailed their heads over the door instead.

In the late 11th century, William the Conqueror put an end to a rebellion in the north of England by killing every man, boy, and farm animal, and burning down all the farms. The remaining people had to eat the dead bodies to survive.

In China in AD910, a relative of the emperor was killed playing polo. The emperor had the entire opposing team beheaded.

After William the Conqueror's death in 1087, his body swelled up with gas as he started to decompose. On the day of his funeral, his stomach exploded, causing a terrible stench. Unable to close the coffin lid, the bishops conducted one of the fastest royal funerals ever recorded.

On his deathbed in 1099, Spanish knight El Cid ordered his men to fasten his corpse to his warhorse after he died, so he could lead them into battle one last time. When the enemy saw the dead man riding toward them, they fled in terror and the Spanish won the battle.

When the coffin of St Cuthbert was opened 417 years after his death in 687, his body was still fresh and smelled sweet. People thought it was a miracle!

In the 1130s, rebels in China's Yanzhou province clothed monkeys in straw and set them on fire to cause trouble in the Chinese emperor's camp.

Sometimes Saxons cut the heads off their dead relatives before burying them. It was supposed to stop them haunting the living, as without a head they wouldn't be able to find their way back home.

During the 1148 siege of Damascus by the crusaders (Christian warriors trying to recapture the Holy Land from the Muslims), the wife of a dead Arab archer picked up his bow and took his place. Her arrows struck the crusaders' standard-bearer and commander, leading to their defeat.

A cowardly soldier who wouldn't fight on a crusade could expect to have his hand pierced right through with a red-hot spike.

A nasty torture device used in the Middle Ages was a metal boot. The victim's foot was put into the boot and it was filled with boiling oil.

In 1191 around 2,700 Muslim prisoners were massacred by English king Richard the Lionheart's army to punish Saladin (the ruler of Syria and Egypt) for his non-payment of a ransom. It was one of the great atrocities of the crusades.

King John of England had an effective way of dealing with difficult bishops – he pinned one under a heavy sheet of lead and left him to starve to death.

In 1212 a shepherd boy called Nicholas of Cologne led a children's crusade to convert Muslims to Christianity. He led his young followers across the Alps into Italy, but the 7,000 children died of disease and starvation before reaching Jerusalem.

Genghis Khan founded a mighty Mongolian empire in the early 13th century. People were so scared of him, that when his army besieged Beijing in 1215, around 60,000 girls threw themselves to their deaths from the city walls rather than face capture.

Samurai swords were rated for sharpness by how many (dead) human bodies they could slice through in one go. The best swords scored a rating of five bodies.

When Genghis Khan laid siege to one city, he demanded 1,000 cats and 10,000 swallows from the inhabitants. He then tied flaming cloths to their tails and set the animals free, setting fire to the city as they went.

In 1190 a troubador (musical poet) fell in love with a married woman. Her husband sent the troubador away on a crusade where he was shot with a poisoned arrow. With his dying breath, the troubador asked a friend to send his heart to his love, but her husband intercepted it, cooked it, and fed it to his wife.

In 13th-century England, someone who had stolen goods worth more than a shilling (five pence/eight cents) could have their head chopped off!

According to legend, when Genghis Khan died in 1227, he was buried beneath a tree near his birthplace. His soldiers killed all witnesses to the funeral (including animals) then killed themselves, so that no living being could know the tomb's location.

A cure for warts in 1250 was to cut off the head of an eel, rub its blood on the warts, and then bury the eel's head. The theory was that as the eel head rotted, the warts would disappear!

Medieval cities were filthy places! In 1281, it took a gang of men a week to clear 20 tonnes (22 tons) of filth from the cesspit (a dumping ground for human sewage) outside London's Newgate Prison.

Relics of saints were so highly valued in the Middle Ages that when holy woman Elisabeth of Thuringia died in 1231, a crowd quickly dismembered her body and stole her bones in anticipation that she would soon be made a saint. She *was* made a saint, but still, that's no excuse...

The French were not the first to use the guillotine. Between 1286 and 1650 the *Halifax gibbet* operated in Halifax, England. It had a blade that was released by men pulling on a rope. The blade would then drop, decapitating the victim.

After her coronation in 1286, Queen Margaret, aged 7, suffered terrible seasickness on the way across the North Sea and died without ever setting foot on the Scottish mainland.

Chinese emperor Hung Wu's harshness was legendary. He had so many people executed that it became customary for government officials to say their last goodbyes to their families if they were summoned for a meeting with him!

In 1287, Mongolian leader Kublai Khan killed a rival by having him wrapped in a carpet and thrown about violently. What a way to go!

A group known as flagellants believed the Black Death was a punishment from God. As penance for their sins, they went from town to town, chanting hymns and whipping themselves with metal-studded straps.

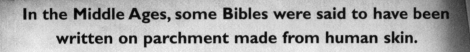

In the Middle Ages, some Bibles were said to have been written on parchment made from human skin.

Fleas living on rats spread bubonic plague – if an infected flea bit you you'd catch it and would probably die soon after. It could also be spread through the air by infected peoples' coughs.

People who developed horribly painful buboes (swellings) were the lucky plague victims – they had a small chance of recovering. The unlucky ones died before any buboes formed, sometimes in a few minutes.

Sir William Wallace, the Scottish rebel leader, had a terrible death after being captured in 1305. He was half-strangled by hanging and then had his intestines cut out! Finally, he was beheaded and his body was cut into four parts.

During a typical medieval siege, missiles thrown by catapults occasionally included rotten food, dead horses, and even captured soldiers.

In 1347 a Mongolian army used a catapult to hurl plague victims into the enemy city of Caffa. They hoped the citizens would catch the plague and be easier to defeat. It was a pretty gruesome weapon!

The Black Death killed very few Mongolian nomads (people with no fixed home). They spent a lot of time with horses and the fleas that carried the plague hated the smell of horses!

Medieval pastimes in England included bearbaiting, bullbaiting, and cockfighting. People would poke the animals with sharp sticks or set dogs on them to make them fight. People would bet on the animal they thought would win.

To punish a revolt in Persia, Mongol leader Tamerlane had the entire population massacred. He left behind a pyramid of 70,000 skulls piled up outside the city walls.

Perfumes made from flowers, oils, and spices were very popular during the Middle Ages. They were an easy solution for people who could not bathe.

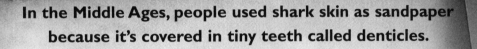

In the Middle Ages, people used shark skin as sandpaper because it's covered in tiny teeth called denticles.

A plague of drunkenness spread through many European towns in the mid 14th century. Many people thought that alcohol would protect them against the Black Death. It didn't.

In 1348 over a million pilgrims held a mass prayer meeting in Rome to combat the plague. Sadly, it spread rapidly through the crowd and fewer than ten percent of the pilgrims lived to return home.

When the mistress of Prince Pedro of Portugal, Inés de Castro, was murdered in 1355, he had her body preserved. When he became king, he had her exhumed and placed on a throne beside him at the coronation feast. Nobles and clergy had to kiss the corpse's hand.

In 1358 there were only four public toilets in the whole of London, England. The largest, on London Bridge, emptied straight into the River Thames.

When the Mongol conqueror, Tamerlane, besieged the city of Sivas in Turkey, he promised not to spill a drop of the residents' blood if they surrendered. The citizens agreed and he kept his word – sort of ... 4,000 Armenians were burned alive, all the Christians were strangled or drowned, and others were trampled to death. The Turks were safe though, as Tamerlane had Turkish relatives!

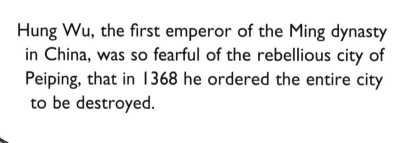

Hung Wu, the first emperor of the Ming dynasty in China, was so fearful of the rebellious city of Peiping, that in 1368 he ordered the entire city to be destroyed.

Between 1370 and 1405, the Mongol leader Tamerlane ordered a tower to be constructed using live men, heaped on top of one another and cemented together with bricks and mortar.

The stepped Aztec pyramids on which human sacrifices took place had channels for the blood to run down, right next to the stairs.

In European cities in the Middle Ages, a drainage channel ran down the middle of the street and all kinds of stuff would be thrown into it: the contents of chamber pots and lavatories, the innards from animals slaughtered for meat, and anything else yucky that was lying around!

In 1425 when she was 17 years old, Joan of Arc freed the French city of Orleans from the English in just nine days. She was captured by the English two years later and burned at the stake as a witch because she claimed the voices of saints had directed her.

Many people in Europe believed the Black Death was spread by "bad air" and thought they could protect themselves by inhaling strong smells. Some sniffed bunches of fragrant herbs, but others crouched for hours over cesspits, breathing in the stench. Rotten!

Leonardo da Vinci produced one of the first textbooks on human anatomy. He cut up the corpses of criminals and sketched them. He also found time to do a spot of painting ... among his works is the *Mona Lisa*, the most famous painting of all time!

Vlad the Impaler ruled Wallachia (present-day Romania) from 1456 to 1462. When 55 Turkish ambassadors refused to remove their hats in his presence, he had their hats nailed to their heads.

The Spanish Inquisition was formed in 1481 and operated officially until 1834 to enforce the laws of the Catholic Church and get rid of heretics (those opposed to the views of the church). The Inquisition executed thousands of people and tortured many more.

In 1471 a court in Switzerland sentenced a chicken to death for laying an egg that they didn't like the look of!

The Italian philosopher Marsilio Ficino (1433–99) recorded that some people would sell elderly people their blood. The old patients sucked it directly from the seller's veins, as medicine.

In the Aztec festival of Tlacaxipehualiztli ("the flaying of men") a sacrificial victim was skinned alive and then a warrior would dress in the skin.

Tortures used by the Spanish Inquisition included the *garrucha*, in which the accused was suspended from the ceiling by a pulley with weights tied to the ankles, often dislocating the victim's arms and legs.

In 1487 the Aztecs of central Mexico sacrificed 20,000 people in four days. The queues of victims, in four lines, were over 3 km (1.8 miles) long.

Those found guilty of heresy by the Spanish Inquisition could be burned at the stake. Around 2,000 people were executed between 1481 and 1490.

An early attempt at a blood transfusion took place in 1492 to try and save the life of Pope Innocent VIII. The blood of three boys was given to him through his mouth. They didn't know much about blood circulation at the time – the pope died and so did the three boys.

Mongol leader Tamerlane played polo with the skulls of people he had killed in battle.

During the Third Crusade in 1191, English king Richard the Lionheart ordered his men to throw 100 beehives over the walls of the besieged city of Acre. The terrified people surrendered immediately.

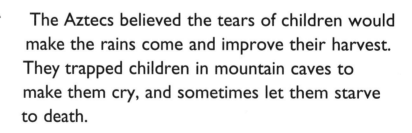

The Aztecs believed the tears of children would make the rains come and improve their harvest. They trapped children in mountain caves to make them cry, and sometimes let them starve to death.

Brides first carried bouquets of flowers in the 16th century to cover up their nasty body smell!

A 16th-century cure for jaundice (liver disease) was to drink a beer containing nine head lice each morning. It might not have cured the jaundice, but it must have got rid of all the head lice!

The Tudor dynasty held the throne in England between 1485 and 1603. It was a time of conflict and rebellion. Criminals faced harsh punishments such as being hanged, burned alive, whipped, branded with a hot iron, or being chained up and pelted with rotten food!

The worst earthquake in history occurred in 1556 in China's Shansi Province, killing 830,000 people.

Tudor King Henry VIII reigned over England from 1509 until his death and married six times. The lucky wives escaped with divorce – two had their heads chopped off!

King Francis I of France who ruled between 1515 and 1547 always journeyed with a small piece of an ancient Egyptian mummy! He used it as a medicine to soothe bruises.

When Ivan the Terrible found out his sixth wife was having an affair, he had her boyfriend impaled on a spike and left to die outside her bedroom window.

To help babies with the pain of teething, a Tudor mother might rub a dead hare on the baby's gums.

In Tudor England, many women wore a lead-based white paste on their faces that literally ate away their skin. They also put poisonous juices from the deadly nightshade plant into their eyes to make their pupils bigger. They must have looked lovely...

Henry VIII carried his own portable toilet with him wherever he went. The "royal stool" was a large box with a feather-padded seat on the lid and a potty inside.

A Tudor cure for gout (a painful illness of the joints) was to boil a red-haired dog in oil, mix in some worms, pig marrow, and herbs and then spread the smelly mixture wherever it hurt!

Under the reign of Henry VIII, around 70,000 people were executed. That's a lot of heads rolling on the floor!

In the 1500s, an entire family would use the same bathwater. The baby would go in last of all, when it was really dirty!

European executioners in the 16th and 17th centuries often wore grotesque iron masks that made them look scary – as if being executed wasn't scary enough already!

Tudor people believed that if they wore fur, any fleas would jump off them and on to the fur instead!

England's Elizabeth I almost died of smallpox in 1562. She survived, but was left with big scars on her face, so she wore a thick, white paste to cover them up.

In 1531 chef Richard Roose was sentenced to death for poisoning members of an English bishop's household. He was dropped into a pot of water hanging over a fire in the town square. It took two hours for the water to boil and kill him.

Henry VIII's second wife, Anne Boleyn, was believed to have had eleven fingers and three breasts.

Ivan the Terrible became the first *tsar* (king) of Russia in 1547. He was poisoned and killed while playing a game of chess in 1584.

The bodies of sacrificial victims in 16th-century central Mexico were fed to the snakes that guarded the holy Aztec temples.

After his execution in 1535, English statesman and scholar Sir Thomas More's head was stuck on a pole at London Bridge. More's daughter paid the bridge keeper to knock it down. She caught it, took it home, and kept it. When she died, she was buried with it.

When Anne Boleyn was beheaded in 1536 on the grounds of treason, there was no coffin provided for her. Her body was stuck in an old arrow chest with the head tucked beneath the arm.

In 1540 Henry VIII got engaged to Anne of Cleves without even meeting her, he just looked at her portrait. When he met her, he found her very ugly, but he went ahead with the ceremony – five months after the wedding, however, he had the marriage declared invalid.

Ivan the Terrible's marriage to his seventh wife lasted just one day. Discovering she already had a boyfriend, he had his new bride drowned.

Mary Queen of Scots who reigned in Scotland between 1542 and 1567, kept a "unicorn's horn" with her throughout her 19-year imprisonment in England, dipping it into her food to test for poison. It was really the horn of a narwhal, a sea mammal with a long tusk.

The night before Henry VIII's fifth wife, Catherine Howard, was executed, she asked for the chopping block to be brought to her cell in the Tower of London. She spent the night rehearsing putting her head on the block so there would be a clean cut on the first stroke.

When he died in 1547, Henry VIII weighed over 182 kg (400 lbs). He was constantly breathless and purple in the face. Ulcers on his swollen legs had to be dressed several times a day and gave off a terrible smell.

Mary I of England – known as "Bloody Mary" – executed more than 200 Protestants during her short reign.

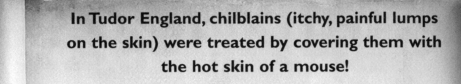

In Tudor England, chilblains (itchy, painful lumps on the skin) were treated by covering them with the hot skin of a mouse!

Lady Jane Grey (the Queen of England for just nine days in 1533) was beheaded along with her husband and father in 1554, once the throne had passed to her successor. Her father's mummified head is still on display in the church of St Botolph Aldgate in London.

The Innuit practice of tattooing was first recorded in 1576, although it had been going on since 1500BC. Tattoo artists were women, who stitched the tattoo into the skin with a stain made with soot, graphite, and urine.

The first known victim of the "the rack" was Cuthbert Simpson, who was tortured for being a Protestant during the reign of England's "Bloody Mary" (Queen Mary I). His hands and feet were tied to rollers and turned opposite ways until his joints popped and he died.

Plague outbreaks were common around Europe in the 16th and 17th centuries. One "cure" that people tried was to hold a cockerel's bottom on a plague sore for as long as possible. If the cockerel died, you had to get another, split it in half while still alive and put that on the sore. This was very economical (two people could be treated with the second cockerel!) but sadly never worked...

When the Earl of Oxford, Edward de Vere, accidentally passed wind while bowing before Queen Elizabeth I, he was so embarrassed that he left court for seven years. On his return, Elizabeth greeted him by saying: "My Lord, I had forgot the fart!"

After a dispute with the city of Novgorod in 1570, Ivan the Terrible ordered the torture and death of every citizen. Many had their fingernails, tongues, hands, ears, or ribs torn out with red-hot pincers.

Artists in the 16th century sometimes added powdered Egyptian mummy to their paint, believing it would stop the surface from cracking when it was dry.

Elizabeth Bathory was a sadistic Hungarian countess who liked to torture young women in the early 1600s. One of her entertainments was to place them in her courtyard on a freezing night and pour water over them to turn them into statues of ice.

Sawney Bean, his wife, 8 sons, and 32 grandchildren lived in a cave in Scotland in the late 16th century. Over a 25-year period, they kidnapped more than 1,000 local people and took them back to their cave where they cut them up and ate them.

When the Egyptian government stopped the export of mummies in the late 16th century, locals set up mummy factories that mummified people who had recently died, and sold them instead!

When King James VI of Scotland learned of the cannibal Bean family, he sent 400 men with dogs to hunt them down. They were captured and taken in chains to Edinburgh where they were executed without trial.

A type of moss that grows on human skulls was popular for nosebleeds in the 17th century. To avoid being cheated by people selling any old moss, rich people would buy an entire skull with the moss still in place.

In March 1658, the famous London diarist Samuel Pepys (1633–1703) had a bladder stone the size of a tennis ball removed without any pain relief – four strong men had to hold him down! Every year on the anniversary of this operation, Pepys toasted his kidney stone (kept in a bottle at home) with a glass of wine.

Oliver Cromwell's embalmed head is now hidden in a secret location in Sidney Sussex College, Cambridge, England. Only two people at any time know where it is – when one dies, another person is told...

King Charles II of England, who reigned between 1660 and 1685, was a strong supporter of "corpse medicine" – he made a distillation from a human skull in his own laboratory, and was dependent on it during his final illness. The very fact that it *was* his final illness suggests that it didn't work very well...

In 1665, the Great Plague broke out in London, killing 80,000 people.

In 1666 a terrible fire destroyed 80 percent of London, but the death toll was very low – perhaps only about ten people lost their lives.

The first successful blood transfusion took place on 15 June 1667, when the blood of a sheep was transfused into a teenage boy. The boy survived, but there is no record of what happened to the sheep...

Following his execution in 1618, Sir Walter Raleigh's wife kept his embalmed head in a red leather bag for 29 years. She even carried it around with her until it got too smelly...

King Charles II of England (1630–85) used to rub himself all over with dust made from powdered Egyptian mummies, in the belief that the greatness of the pharaohs would rub off on him.

An 18th-century vaccination against smallpox was made by taking pus from the sores on a dairymaid's hands and rubbing it onto a scratch on the patient's arm.

Executioners earned extra money by cutting off the heads from people who had been hung, cleaning them of flesh and brains, and selling them medicine.

In 18th-century England, people who had committed suicide were buried at a crossroads with a stake through their hearts. The crossroads were supposed to confuse a ghost so that it couldn't find its way home and the stake was to keep the body in the ground!

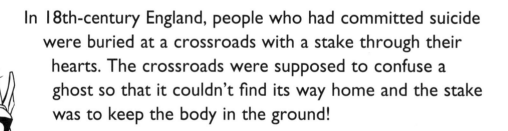

Blackbeard the pirate met his end on in November 1718 when Robert Maynard of the British Navy was sent to capture him. Blackbeard jumped aboard Maynard's ship, where he received five gunshot wounds and at least 20 sword wounds before he fell down, dead.

In the 18th century, doctors wanted to cut up dead bodies to find out how they worked. It was illegal to dissect dead people, so they had to pay grave robbers to steal newly-buried bodies, or take hanged criminals from the gallows.

In 1741 Arctic explorers found that the local people decorated their bodies with piercings threaded with bones, worn through the chin, forehead, or nose.

A common pirate punishment was keelhauling. Victims were tied to a rope and dragged under the ship, then up the other side. They emerged half drowned, with their skin shredded by the barnacles that grew on the ship's hull.

Dick Turpin's career as a violent highway robber ended when he was arrested for shooting his landlord's cockerel. A former schoolmaster recognized him while he was awaiting trial and he was hanged in York, England, in 1739.

The War of Jenkins' Ear between England and Spain erupted in 1739, after the Spanish cut off the ear of Captain Robert Jenkins. It was a warning to English traders to keep away from their American colonies.

In 1789 hanging, rather than burning, became the official method of execution in Britain.

In 1758 British settlers tried to infect Native American tribes by giving them blankets from dead smallpox patients.

Saws used by 19th-century surgeons to amputate arms and legs had large notches cut into the blades so that they didn't completely clog up with flesh and gristle.

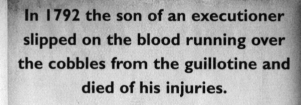

In 1792 the son of an executioner slipped on the blood running over the cobbles from the guillotine and died of his injuries.

William Carlisle of Rhode Island, USA, was convicted of forgery in 1771. He was sentenced to have both ears cut off and to be branded with the letter "R" for "rogue" on both cheeks.

The guillotine was intended to make execution painless.

A blood-draining alternative to leeches, used by 19th-century doctors, was an instrument called a *scarificator* (a bit like a small rolling pin with six blades). As it was rolled over the skin it made six cuts, in nice, neat rows.

At the battle of Waterloo in 1815, looters stole teeth from dead bodies and sold them to rich people to use as false teeth. "Waterloo teeth" were a huge hit among European high society.

The first victim of the guillotine was highwayman Nicolas Pelletier, who was executed in Paris in April 1792.

King Charles I of England (who was beheaded in 1649) was dug up for an autopsy in 1813. The royal surgeon, Sir Henry Halford, stole a bone from the king's spine and for many years, Halford used it to hold salt on his dining table. How rude!

The poor, particularly children, were often stitched into their clothes for the whole winter as it was never warm enough to take them off, even in bed. The clothes would only be removed in the spring – they must have needed a wash by then!

Spanish artist Francisco de Goya, who died in 1828, may have been killed by his own paint. Goya used poisonous mercury and lead in his paints, which slowly built up in his body.

In the 1830s, a British ship arrived at a port in China and fired a cannon as a greeting. Tragically a bystander was killed by one of the cannon shots and the ship's captain was forced to hand over the gunner, who was promptly strangled.

The first fatal railway accident occurred in 1831, when the boiler exploded on America's first passenger locomotive *The Best Friend of Charleston*.

Shaka, leader of the South African Zulu tribe from 1818 to 1828, didn't trust his witch-finders, so he set them a test. He smeared blood on his own house and told them to find the witch who did it. When they found 300 "guilty" people Shaka had the witch-finders put to death.

One 19th-century American highwayman asked for a copy of his memoirs to be bound in his own skin after his execution.

Around 1850, Baron Heurteloup invented an artificial leech, rather like a hypodermic syringe, for drawing out blood without the need to maintain an army of live leeches!

Despite his terrifying appearance, James Lucas became a national curiosity. People came from far away to see the "dirtiest man in England" – he never washed and gradually his body went black with grease and grime.

A cholera epidemic in London (1853–4) killed nearly 11,000 people. It resulted in the discovery that cholera comes from dirty water – after that London was given proper sewers.

Small children were sent to clean chimneys because they could easily fit up a narrow chimney stack. To toughen up their knees and elbows, they had to rub strong salt water into their skin while sitting very near a hot fire. Their employer would stand over them with a cane to make sure they were close enough.

A Chinese torture chair from the 19th century has blades sticking up from the armrests and seat, and sticking out from the back. It would be impossible to sit on it without being stabbed – your own weight would push the blades into your flesh.

The tenth English duke of Hamilton was so interested in Egyptian mummies he got a doctor to mummify him and put him into a stone tomb, when he died in 1852, just like a pharaoh!

In 1854 Florence Nightingale arrived in Scutari, Turkey, to work as a nurse during the Crimean War. She soon discovered that amputated limbs were left outside for pigs to eat.

English naturalists William and Frank Buckland (father and son) tried eating various things from nature, including stewed flies, mice on toast, and a mole! Tasty…

In 1859 the *Saint Paul* left Hong Kong on its voyage to Australia. It was shipwrecked on the way, and all but one of the 326 passengers on board were roasted and eaten by cannibals on the island of Rossel, Papua New Guinea.

When Indian soldiers mutinied in 1857 at the start of the first Indian war of Independence, the British responded savagely. One punishment was to strap a rebel across the mouth of a cannon and fire it.

In the summer of 1858, the smell of untreated sewage almost overwhelmed the people of London. It was so bad that Parliament had to close down!

Leeches were still used for draining blood during the 19th century. Special "leech tubes" were used to direct small leeches into awkward areas, such as inside the ears.

In 19th-century London, wealthy members of society held "mummy unwrapping parties" – they were extremely popular and became the hottest tickets in town!

American inventor William Bullock helped to revolutionize the printing industry with his web rotary printing press, developed in 1863. In a bizarre accident, Bullock was killed by his own invention when he became caught up in one of his machines.

"They couldn't hit an elephant at this dist…" were the last words of General John Sedgwick, killed in battle during the American Civil War in 1864.

Alfred Nobel invented dynamite in 1867. He later deeply regretted it because of the explosive's use in warfare and used the fortune he earned from his invention to set up the Nobel Peace Prize.

Public hangings were stopped in England in 1868. They were so popular that many people were hurt or killed in the crush to see the action!

The world's first ever traffic light was installed in December 1868 outside the Houses of Parliament in London. Unfortunately it exploded a month later, injuring the policeman operating it.

During the siege of Paris in 1870–1, the city ran out of food. Restaurants served cat, dog, and rat!

Ancient Egyptian mummies were used as fuel in the 19th century. There were so many that they were burned to power trains. Poor people in Egypt burned mummy bandages to heat their houses.

In the 19th century, prisoners were holed up in filthy, crowded ships on the river Thames. In the daytime they were let out to do horrible tasks, like cleaning away sewage.

The two half-sisters of playwright Oscar Wilde burned to death at a party in 1871. They walked too close to a fire and their huge crinolines (petticoats) caught light.

Englishwoman Mary Ann Cotton was hanged in 1873 for poisoning at least 15 people with arsenic. She got away with it by moving around the country to areas where she wasn't known, before killing again.

In the early 1870s, the western frontier town of Palisade, Nevada, USA, was famed as the roughest, toughest town in the Wild West! Whenever a train pulled into the station, passengers were shocked to see gunfights, stabbings, and bank robberies ... but in fact they were all staged to maintain the town's reputation!

William Buckland liked exotic food. Among the meals he tried were elephant's trunk soup, roast giraffe, and panther chops. He even tried earwigs once, but complained they tasted rather bitter.

Australian outlaw Ned Kelly protected himself with a homemade metal helmet and waistcoat during a shootout with police in June 1880. He forgot to cover his legs though and was shot there instead.

Flogging (whipping) was allowed as punishment in the British army until 1881. Other European armies gave it up long before then.

In Mongolia in the 19th century, prisoners were kept in coffins for years and years as punishment.

When trying to remove an assassin's bullet from the chest of the American President James Garfield in 1881, doctors poking their fingers into the wound accidentally punctured the president's liver.

In 1888 an Egyptian farmer discovered an ancient cat cemetery containing 10,000 cat mummies. The entire haul was shipped to Liverpool in England, where the mummies were ground up and sold as fertilizer.

Jack the Ripper mutilated and killed a number of women in the Whitechapel area of London in 1888. The identity of the murderer is still unproven to this day.

In Rhode Island, USA, in 1892, Mercy Brown's father had her body dug up after her death, burned her heart, and mixed it into a drink for her brother. He believed she was a vampire and was killing his son, who was actually dying of tuberculosis.

In Victorian Britain, people who couldn't afford a proper burial were buried in paupers' graveyards. These were so crowded that often the bodies poked up through the ground and gave off a horrible smell.

"Mountain man" John Johnson (1824–1900) married a Native American woman of the Flathead tribe. When she was killed and scalped by another tribe, Johnson began hunting down its members in search of revenge. He scalped them and ate their livers raw.

Archduke Karl Ludwig of Austria was deeply religious. On a pilgrimage to the Holy Land in 1896, he insisted on drinking from the River Jordan, but it poisoned him and he died.

In the 19th century, mummy bandages were often used to make paper. This became illegal after an outbreak of the deadly disease cholera in America was traced to mummy-paper that had been used to wrap food!

In 1897 Belgian Count Karnice-Karnicki invented a mechanism that could detect chest movements occurring in a "corpse" in a coffin. It set off warning bells and raised a flag over the grave to alert people to the premature burial.

The influenza pandemic of 1918–19 was the worst of all time, killing approximately 25 million. That's more than the number killed in World War I.

In 1935 Dr Egas Moniz of Portugal developed the surgical procedure of lobotomy. A mallet was used to drive an ice pick through the top of the eye socket to cut the lobes at the front of the brain, as a way to cure mental illness. It sounds more like torture!

Until the 1940s, the Mundurucú tribe of the Amazon tattooed all children until the age of 16, adding stripes, bands, and patterns slowly over time, until the entire body was tattooed to look like a bird.

Henry Wellcome, founder of the Wellcome Foundation (a medical research charity since 1936) made a large collection of medical curiosities, including pieces of human skin with interesting tattoos, instruments of torture, and scary medical instruments.

The worst plane crash in history occurred on the runway! Two Boeing 747 jumbo jets collided in Tenerife in March 1977. Nearly 600 people were killed.

In March 1974, Britain's *Daily Mirror* became the first mass-circulation newspaper to picture a naked streaker on its front page.

The Khmer Rouge regime which ruled Cambodia from 1975 to 1979 killed between 1.7 and 2.3 million people. Many victims were forced to dig their own graves before being killed with hammers, spades, or sharpened bamboo sticks to save bullets.

In 1977 American forest ranger Roy Cleveland Sullivan achieved a world record he might not have wished for. In that year he was struck by lightning for a seventh time – and survived!

The final victim of the guillotine was murderer Hamida Djandoubi, who was beheaded in Marseilles, France, in September 1977.

Incredibly Strange History Quiz

HISTORY QUIZ 1

1 What did hideous Chinese lord Shang Yang do to someone who failed to report a crime in 356 BC?

a) he cut off their toes
b) he cut them in two
c) he cut off their heads

2 Which vile disease did British settlers try to give to Native Americans in 1758?

a) cowpox
b) chickenpox
c) smallpox

1 SLIME BONUS POINT

3 In ancient Rome, when a criminal was beheaded where was the head thrown?

a) into the sewer
b) at the public
c) into a basket

4 How was one ancient Egyptian charioteer punished for drink driving?

a) he was run over with his chariot
b) he was drowned in a vat of beer
c) he was nailed to a tavern door

5 What was the coded message given by the Allied armies on D-Day in 1944 when they landed in France?

a) John has a long moustache
b) John has a pipe in his pocket
c) John has a bee in his underpants

6 What unusual food did people eat during the siege of Leningrad in Russia, which took place 1941–42?

a) cardboard
b) rats
c) each other

REALLY HORRID!

8 What did a Tudor mother sometimes rub on a baby's gums to help with the pain of teething?

a) a dead hare
b) a wet sardine
c) a frozen mouse

7 Which household item did the Romans put urine in?

a) dishwashing liquid
b) soap
c) toothpaste

9 What happened to the head of King Charles I after he was executed for treason in 1649?

a) it was boiled in a pot
b) it was sewn back on
c) it was used as a candle holder

1 SLIME BONUS POINT

10 How long did it take for the blade of a guillotine to fall and slice off the victim's head?

a) less than a second
b) about 30 seconds
c) about 1 minute

Answers on page 252

HISTORY QUIZ 2

1 Who died on the toilet in 1760?

a) Oliver Cromwell
b) Queen Elizabeth I
c) King George II

2 What hideous thing did Irene, mother of Byzantine emperor Constantine VI, do to her son?

a) she blinded him
b) she tortured him
c) she killed him

3 In which part of the house did people in ancient Jericho bury their decomposing relatives?

a) under the floor
b) in the walls
c) in the bathroom

4 How did Heraclitus, the ancient Greek philosopher, try to cure himself of dropsy (water on the lungs)?

a) he ate rotten eggs
b) he buried himself in cow dung
c) he bathed in frog spawn

5 When King Charlemagne died in AD814, he was mummified. Where was he seated for 400 years?

a) on the royal toilet
b) on the royal bed
c) on the royal throne

1 SLIME BONUS POINT

6 When Captain Robert Jenkins showed his severed ear in the British Parliament in 1739, what happened?

a) everyone fainted
b) it started a war
c) a dog ran over and ate it

7 In which period were chilblains (itchy, painful skin lumps) treated by covering them with the hot skin of a mouse?

a) Roman times
b) Saxon times
c) Tudor times

8 What truly hideous habit did the ancient Assyrians have?

a) they boiled enemies alive
b) they burned enemies alive
c) they skinned enemies alive

9 In 1858 what horrible pong could the people of London smell for the whole summer?

a) horse poop
b) raw sewage
c) rotting pigeons

10 In which country has there been a festival every year since 1994 where people throw tomatoes at each other?

a) Argentina
b) Spain
c) Peru

Answers on page 252

HISTORY QUIZ 3

1 One Roman concoction included powdered snake and goats' blood. What was it for?

a) removing earwax
b) scrubbing your feet
c) removing body hair

2 What did the Saxons sometimes do to their dead relatives before burying them?

a) chop off their heads
b) chop off their fingers
c) chop off their toes

3 In 1854 during the Battle of Balaclava in Russia, what did freezing British soldiers burn to keep warm?

a) their pants
b) bars of chocolate
c) toilet roll

4 What did the lead-based paste Tudor women wore do to their skin?

a) it gave them blood blisters
b) it ate away their flesh
c) it gave them giant boils

5 For how long was Lady Jane Grey Queen of England before she was beheaded in 1553?

a) 9 days
b) 19 days
c) 109 days

1 SLIME BONUS POINT

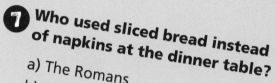

6 **What did the Brazilian Wari tribe do up until the 1960s?**

a) eat humans
b) drill holes in people's skulls
c) sleep on beds of needles

7 **Who used sliced bread instead of napkins at the dinner table?**

a) The Romans
b) Medieval monks
c) The ancient Greeks

8 **What did listeners believe was really happening during a radio broadcast of HG Wells' "War of the Worlds" in 1938?**

a) evil aliens were invading Earth
b) crazed zombies were attacking everyone
c) killer bees were destroying the planet

9 **Who died a gruesome death in 3030BC when they were stomped on by a hippopotamus?**

a) Pharaoh Hor-Aha
b) Pharaoh Tutankhamun
c) Queen Nefertiti

10 **What was King Edmund II of England sitting on when he was murdered in 1016?**

a) a toadstool
b) a toilet
c) a horse

1 SLIME BONUS POINT

Answers on page 252

HISTORY QUIZ 4

1 Why did cave people mix up warm animal blood with gooey plant extracts?

a) to make hair dye
b) to make cave paintings
c) to make hot drinks

1 SLIME BONUS POINT

2 In 1917 three Portuguese children claimed they saw a holy vision. What punishment were they threatened with?

a) burning at the stake
b) drowning in the river
c) being boiled in oil

3 Richard Roose, chef to a bishop, was put to death for poisoning in 1531. How did he die?

a) he was roasted on a spit
b) he was fried in a vat of oil
c) he was boiled in a pot of water

4 What did Roman king Tarquinius Priscus do to people who had committed suicide, even though they were already dead?

a) he pulled out their fingernails
b) he chopped off their heads
c) he hung them from a cross

5 What did the Aztecs do to the people they sacrificed in 16th-century Mexico?

a) they ate them for dinner
b) they fed them to snakes
c) they made them into shrunken heads

6 What did the ancient Egyptians try to cure with a potion made from a mashed pig's eyeball?

a) stomach ache
b) fever
c) blindness

7 In 11th-century England, what was the punishment for lying while serving on a jury in court?

a) walking on burning coals
b) plunging your hand into boiling water
c) eating a bucketful of maggots

8 William Carlisle of Rhode Island, USA, was convicted of forgery in 1771. What was his punishment?

a) to be branded with a hot iron
b) to walk on burning coals
c) to have his thumbs cut off

REALLY HORRID!

9 What smelly thing did King Henry VIII always take with him in the 16th century?

a) his potty
b) a scoop for his poo
c) his pet skunk

10 What was drilling a hole in a person's skull an ancient French cure for?

a) earache
b) stomach ache
c) headache

1 SLIME BONUS POINT

Answers on page 252

HISTORY QUIZ 5

1 Why did people in the Middle Ages tie smelly sheep bones to their feet?

a) to use them as slippers
b) to cure athlete's foot
c) to use them as ice skates

2 What did the early Romans use for cleaning out smelly bits of food from between their teeth?

a) porcupine quills
b) shark teeth
c) anteater claws

TOO STINKY!

3 What smelly material was used to help build houses in medieval England?

a) pig poop
b) chicken poop
c) rat poop

1 SLIME BONUS POINT

4 In the 19th century, what was the English geologist, William Buckland, said to have eaten?

a) the heart of King Louis XIV
b) the brains of a T. rex
c) the liver of King Charles I

5 When Pope Formosus died in AD96, why was his rotting corpse dug up?

a) to be dissected
b) to be mummified
c) to be put on trial

6 **What did Ivan the Terrible do to his sixth wife when he discovered she had a secret boyfriend?**

a) stuck him on a spike
b) stuck him in the microwave
c) nailed him to a door

7 **What method did the ancient Greek doctor Hippocrates use to work out what was wrong with patients?**

a) he tested their urine
b) he tasted their urine
c) he sniffed their urine

1
SLIME BONUS POINT

8 **Which of these gross events did the Spartans of ancient Greece hold?**

a) nose-picking competitions
b) whipping competitions
c) hedgehog-eating competitions

9 **When the year AD999 came to a close, what were people terrified would happen?**

a) the world would end
b) aliens would invade Earth
c) apes would take over the planet

10 **In which period was it most common to keep a person's skull as a holy relic?**

a) the Middle Ages
b) Victorian times
c) the 20th century

Answers on page 252

HISTORY QUIZ ANSWERS

History Quiz 1

1) b   2) c   3) a   4) c   5) a   6) b   7) c   8) a   9) b   10) a

History Quiz 2

1) c   2) a   3) a   4) b   5) c   6) b   7) c   8) c   9) b   10) b

History Quiz 3

1) c   2) a   3) b   4) b   5) a
6) a   7) c   8) a   9) a   10) b

History Quiz 4

1) b   2) a   3) c   4) c   5) b
6) c   7) b   8) a   9) a   10) c

History Quiz 5

1) c   2) a   3) a   4) a   5) c
6) a   7) b   8) b   9) a   10) a

Incredibly Strange Animal Facts

The vampire finch is so called because of its habit of pecking other birds and feeding on their blood!

Owls swallow their prey (mostly mice and voles) whole. The parts they cannot digest, like fur and bones, are formed into small pellets which the owl vomits up.

Pitohui birds eat a certain type of beetle that makes their skin and feathers poisonous to predators.

Birds that lay their eggs in the nests of other birds often check to see if their eggs are being cared for. If their eggs have been removed, the birds vandalize the nest, killing any other eggs or chicks.

The shrike got its nickname "the butcher bird" from its habit of impaling its prey onto spikes to hold it still, so that the shrike can devour it more easily.

Chocolate, avocado, and mushrooms are poisonous to parrots.

Penguin urine accounts for nearly 3 percent of the ice in Antarctic glaciers.

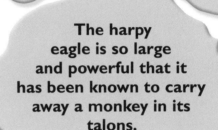

The harpy eagle is so large and powerful that it has been known to carry away a monkey in its talons.

The southern giant petrel likes to vomit smelly stomach oils and regurgitated food at predators or nosy humans.

In January 2009, a US Airways flight crash-landed on the Hudson River in New York. A bird had been sucked into one of its engines causing power failure. Amazingly, no one was harmed!

Did you know that not all blood is red like ours? Lobster blood is blue and insect blood is yellow.

Over 100 million birds die annually in the USA by accidentally crashing into glass windows. There are some pretty stupid birds out there!

In 1920's Britain, people used to clean their chimneys by dropping live chickens down them. The chickens would end up part-plucked and, if the chimney was still warm, part-cooked, too.

Vultures are able to spot a carcass around the size of an average dog from 6.4 km (4 miles) away on open plains.

After humans colonized the island of Mauritius in 1600, the dodo – a bird native to the island – became extinct just 100 years later.

A mosquito can drink one and a half times its own weight in blood in a single meal.

Fearsome driver ants move in such massive colonies that they can strip the flesh from any animal they come across down to the bone. They have been known to completely devour wounded lions and crocodiles.

When a mosquito bites you, it's the enzymes in its saliva that cause you to itch, not the bite itself.

When it's time for dinner, a spider traps its prey before injecting it with a chemical that turns the bug's insides to mush. The spider then sucks out the liquid like a bug milkshake.

Queen termites lay an egg every second for up to 50 years.

The myth that garlic wards off vampires may not be true, but it does help to repel mosquitoes.

The record for the world's heaviest spider was a giant bird-eating spider found in Suriname in 1965. It weighed 122 g (4 oz). That's about the same as a large apple!

Geckos clean their eyes using their tongues ... a bit like windscreen wipers!

To defend their territory, guard termites sometimes make themselves explode to scare off attackers.

The caterpillar of the polyphemus moth chomps its way through 86,000 times its own birth weight in food in the first 56 days of its life. That would be the same as a human baby munching through about 150,000 burgers!

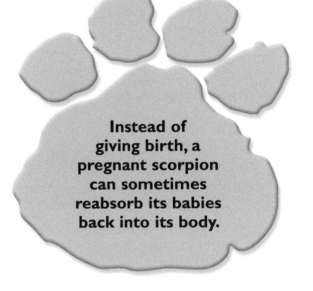

Instead of giving birth, a pregnant scorpion can sometimes reabsorb its babies back into its body.

The number of mosquitoes that hatch during the Arctic summer is so great that their swarms blot out the sun.

Even after it has been cut off, an octopus tentacle will carry on wriggling for some time.

A patch of rainforest soil around the size of this book can contain 10,000 mosquito eggs.

The anglerfish lives in the darkest depths of the sea and has a glowing blob, like a little lantern, dangling in front of its head!

Some leeches have 300 teeth, 100 in each of their three blood-sucking jaws.

A dying barracuda fish will gorge itself on anything that will make its flesh poisonous, such as small creatures and plants. That way, anything that eats the barracuda after it dies will also be killed. Nasty!

A leech will only finish sucking blood when it is five times its original size.

The teeth of a viperfish are half the length of its head, so it can't close its mouth! It has to open its jaws very wide in order to swallow.

A blue whale's tongue can weigh the same as an elephant.

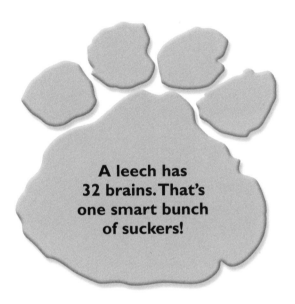

A leech has 32 brains. That's one smart bunch of suckers!

A flea can jump 30,000 times without stopping.

The guts of the African N'gwa caterpillar are so poisonous that tribesmen use them to tip their spears and arrowheads.

In March 2014, a huge huntsman spider jumped out of a charity worker's backpack on her return to the UK after visiting a rainforest in Cameroon. It was described as being "quite feisty" and had an egg sac containing hundreds of babies.

The sting of a tropical cone snail can be fatal to a human being. Luckily, they live underwater so you should be safe in your garden…

In July 1874, a swarm of Rock Mountain locusts flew over Nebraska, covering an area approximately 515,000 sq km (198,600 sq miles).

Cockroaches breed so fast that if a single pair reproduced for a year, with all their babies reproducing as well, there would be ten million of them altogether.

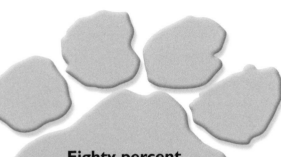

Eighty percent of all living things are nematode worms – found everywhere, including in salt and fresh water, soil, and inside plants and animals.

If two flies were left to reproduce for a year, without any threat from predators, the resulting mass of flies would be the size of planet Earth!

The necrophorus beetle uses the fur of dead animals to build its nest.

You can't feel the bite of a leech because it produces a natural painkiller before latching on. How thoughtful…

The tarantula hawk is actually a wasp! The female wasp attacks and paralyzes a tarantula spider before laying an egg in its body. The hatched wasp then eats the tarantula alive as its first meal.

The fat-tailed scorpion is responsible for most human deaths from scorpion stings. Although its venom is less toxic than that of the deathstalker scorpion, it injects more into its victim.

The Pharaoh ant loves to feast on human wounds and bloody bandages. It's a regular visitor to the hospital…

Locusts travel in swarms of up to 80 million at a time and can cover an area the size of a whole town.

The blood consumed in a single meal can keep a leech alive for up to nine months!

Anteaters, armadillos, bats, duck-billed platypuses, whales, and dolphins are all immune from getting lice.

When Montana mountain goats compete for females, they can butt their heads against each other so hard that the shock can cause their hooves to fall off.

The bite of the Komodo dragon delivers toxins that prevent blood clotting, so their victims often go into shock from rapid blood loss.

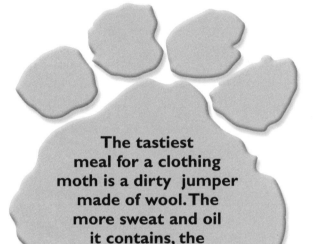

The tastiest meal for a clothing moth is a dirty jumper made of wool. The more sweat and oil it contains, the better.

Just a single bat can eat between 3,000 and 7,000 mosquitoes in a night. A colony of 500 of the flying fiends can munch their way through a quarter of a million bugs in an hour.

In reference books in the Middle Ages in Europe, dragons were listed as real animals!

Driver ants kill their victims not by poison or venom, but by slashing at them with their pincers. They do it in such great numbers that their prey eventually bleeds to death from thousands of tiny cuts.

Blowflies are the first kind of insect attracted to a carcass (the body of a dead animal) following its death.

Some types of botfly lay their eggs on the abdomens of other blood-sucking insects, such as fleas or ticks. When they hatch, the baby botflies burrow into the skin of the animal and suck the poor victim dry as their first meal.

Because maggots have no teeth, they ooze ferment (saliva) from their mouths to liquidize their food before sucking it up.

A female tiger shark carries several babies during pregnancy but only gives birth to one. In the womb, the strongest baby eats the others until it is the only one left.

The Komodo dragon (a lizard) can grow to 3 m (10 ft) in length and can detect food up to 10 km (6 miles) away.

The Argentinian wide-mouthed frog will eat prey as large as itself, sometimes eating to the point of bursting its own stomach.

Ancient Greek dentists used the venom from a stingray's spine to numb the mouth.

You could power two fridges with the electricity produced by a single electric eel.

In just one year, lemon sharks grow more than 24,000 new teeth. That's a full set every two weeks! Who needs to bother with brushing?

When it has eaten as much as it can, a barracuda will herd any remaining fish that it has not eaten into shallow water. It guards them until it is ready to eat again.

Skunks can accurately spray their smelly scent as far as 3 m (10 ft).

Stargazer fish are like super electric eels. As well as delivering electric shocks, they also have two poisonous spines on their backs. Scary!

The viperfish catches its prey by swimming straight toward its target and impaling (spearing) it on its huge teeth.

Chocolate can be deadly to a dog's heart and nervous system. Just a handful is enough to kill a small dog. It's bad for cats too.

Onions are bad for both dogs and cats, causing their red blood cells to burst.

The African black rhinoceros excretes its own weight in dung every 48 hours. That's 682 kg (1,500 lb) a day!

A rabbit's tongue contains 17,000 taste buds. That's 7,000 more than an average human!

Guinea pig meat is always on the menu in Peru and Bolivia, where the animals are bred as food.

A bakery near Frankfurt, Germany, offers tasty treats such as tuna cakes and garlic cookies … just for dogs!

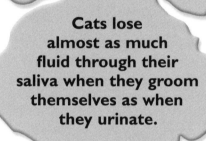

Cats lose almost as much fluid through their saliva when they groom themselves as when they urinate.

The babies of the *boulengerula taitanus* (a worm-like amphibian) actually eat their own mother's skin. The babies use special teeth when born to squirm all over their mother's body and remove her flesh. Somehow the mother usually survives!

In 2005 animal control officers investigated complaints of a foul smell coming from the house of 82-year-old Ruth Kneuven in Virginina, USA. Inside they found nearly 500 cats, more than 100 of which were dead.

Said to be the most expensive in the world, Kopi luwak coffee is made from the undigested coffee beans eaten by palm civet cats of Indonesia. You have to pick the beans from the cat's droppings before you can make a cup…

If you drink water with a leech in it, the tiny bloodsucker can attach to the inside of your mouth or throat and suck you dry from the inside.

The world's largest ant colony was discovered in 2002. The interconnecting nests stretch 5,760 km (3,579 miles) from the Italian Riviera right through into northern Spain. The super-colony is home to several billion ants.

Before synthetic bristles were invented, wild boar hair was used to make toothbrushes.

Locust swarms regularly cause traffic accidents in hot countries. There are so many of the flying insects around that cars often skid on the piles of squashed bugs that litter the highways.

Japanese scientists have bred completely transparent frogs so that they can investigate their internal organs without having to kill and dissect them.

The African zorilla (a type of polecat) could be the smelliest creature on the planet. The stench secreted from its anal glands can be detected up to 1 km (0.5 mile) away.

The first recorded occurence of a frog being sick was when one was taken on a space flight.

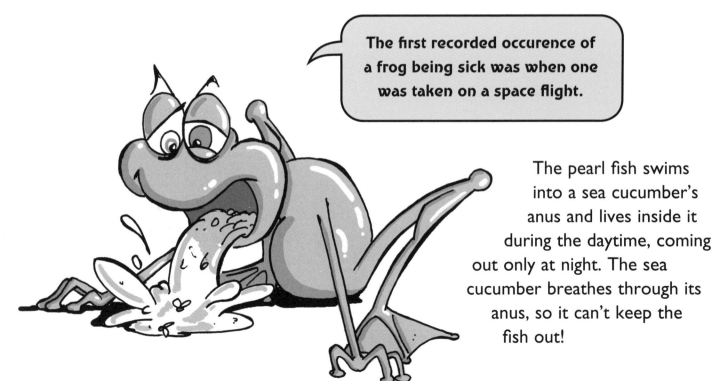

The pearl fish swims into a sea cucumber's anus and lives inside it during the daytime, coming out only at night. The sea cucumber breathes through its anus, so it can't keep the fish out!

Four animals have blue tongues: the black bear, the chow chow dog, the giraffe, and the blue-tongued skink.

Bee venom contains a substance called melittin, which reduces swelling. It's used to treat medical conditions such as arthritis. Bees are pressed on the patient and allowed to sting away!

The vampire bat is only the size of an adult thumb, but its razor-sharp teeth can pierce straight through a cow's skin. It splits open one of the cow's veins and sucks up to five teaspoonfuls of blood in one go.

Blister beetles secrete a poison that leaves a painful blister on the skin of its victim.

A vampire bat needs to eat every day or it will die. If it cannot find food it will flick the cheek of a well-fed bat to make it vomit. The hungry bat then happily munches on the sloppy seconds.

Fungus gnats from New Zealand dribble slime which collects in the roofs of the caves where they live. The gnats can make their bodies llight up to attract insects, which then get caught in the goo before being eaten.

Some stinkbugs are able to spit their smelly goo as far as 30 cm (1 ft). Not bad for a bug often no more than 1.5 cm (½ in) long!

An elephant can produce a 38-kg (83-lb) pile of poop in one go.

Whales vomit every 7 to 10 days to get rid of any indigestible items they may have swallowed.

Artist Chris Ofili from Manchester, England, is known for using elephant dung in many of his creations!

In 2004 children at a nursery in Weston-super-Mare, England, were alarmed to see a three-headed, six-legged, mutant frog creeping out of their pond.

A vulture's stomach contains acids so strong that they can dissolve anything – even flesh containing the fatal anthrax disease, which can kill a human in just a few days.

According to an old Californian law, it is illegal to pile horse manure more than 1.82 m (6 ft) high on any street corner.

Cottonmouth snake venom is very effective at removing bloodstains from white clothes. Although getting the venom may cause even more bloodstains...

The fart of a female southern pine beetle contains a pheromone called frontalin, which attracts male beetles.

A pair of pigs in northern Italy became so enormous that they could not be moved and had to be taken from their sty in pieces. The pigs weighed 200 kg (440 lb) each.

A pond in Hamburg was dubbed "the pond of death" in 2004 when hundreds of toads exploded after being attacked by crows. The unlucky crows scattered toad guts more than 3 m (10 ft) away.

In Illinois in 2008, a dashchund chewed off his owner's big toe as she slept. The owner had nerve damage so she didn't feel anything until it was too late!

Vets at Seneca Park Zoo, USA, had to use a hammer and chisel to remove an infected tooth from a polar bear in 2005. The tooth had been giving the bear bad breath. How they got close enough to find out is a mystery!

Lightning struck a farm in northern Israel in 2004, causing the death of 10,000 chickens. Fried chicken anyone?

The head of a sperm whale contains up to 2.75 tonnes (3 tons) of a substance called spermaceti. It turns hard and waxy while the whale is diving in the cold ocean depths and becomes oilier and more liquid as the whale gets warmer. The oil used to be an ingredient in some types of cosmetics.

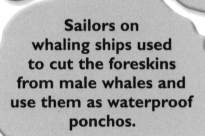

Sailors on whaling ships used to cut the foreskins from male whales and use them as waterproof ponchos.

Cave swiftlets of Southeast Asia make nests from their own saliva. Locals use the dried nests to make the delicacy bird's nest soup – yes, it's a soup made from spit!

When a shark dies, it sinks so slowly to the bottom of the ocean that the salt water almost completely dissolves its corpse. The only parts that don't dissolve or get eaten are its teeth.

The Coopers Nutmeg snail lies hidden in the sand in shallow water until a ray passes by. It then attaches itself to the ray before making a small slash in its victim's skin and feeding on its blood.

Aborigines of Australia dig up the nests of honey ants to eat the tiny critters as a snack. The ants live on sweet foods like sugar and honey and taste very sweet, if a little on the crunchy and wriggly side.

Fire ants are so called because a bite from one feels like a nasty burn on the skin.

Unlucky whales can be infected with sinus flukes. The fist-sized parasites like to live in the whale's airways, occasionally burrowing into their brains, too.

The candiru (an eel-like fish) lives in the Amazon River and is more feared than the pirahna. The transparent fish can smell urine in the water and heads straight for the source. It enters the body of its victim and burrows toward a major blood vessel to feed.

Soldier flies like to lay their eggs in human excrement. The larvae are often found in bathrooms as they crawl up the sewage pipes.

Planarian worms shoot a tube out of their throats which holds down their prey. Then they drip enzymes all over their victim to soften it up before tearing chunks off it to eat.

Fried spiders are regularly eaten as a delicacy in Cambodia. Apparently they taste like nuts.

Bluebottle and greenbottle flies, which are common visitors to our homes, bring with them the bacteria and yuckiness from the rotting meat, carcasses, and animal poop where they lay their eggs.

In the UK alone, domestic cats kill 57 million mammals a year, 27 million birds, and 5 million reptiles and amphibians.

In an American survey, at least 63 percent of dog owners admitted to kissing their dogs. When asked to state where they kissed them, 29 percent listed the place as "other"! Eeewww!

If a venomous Gila monster lizard bites your finger, it won't let go – victims have been known to arrive at hospital with the huge reptile still attached!

The average housefly will only live for about four weeks. No wonder they buzz around so quickly!

It is impossible to filter all traces of fish dander (flaking scales) from our drinking water. Pass the dandruff shampoo...

Dogs like eating cat poop because it's high in protein.

A man in India set a new world record in 2003 by swallowing 200 live earthworms in just over 20 seconds.

Sharks don't have a urinary tract, so they have to urinate straight through their skin.

Giraffes have such long and flexible tongues that they can lick inside their own ears. Nobody knows what they taste like though.

The horned lizard from South America can shoot blood out of its eyes when under attack.

Armadillos produce so much saliva that they have a small pocket at the back of their tongue to store it in.

Chinese scientists have found that common houseflies carry a minimum of 1,941,000 different bacteria on their bodies.

Cows release vast amounts of methane gas every year.

Osedax mucofloris is a slimy sea worm that feeds on whale remains and looks like a flower growing on the bone it's eating. Its name means "bone-eating mucus flower"!

A woodpecker's tongue can be as long as its body! It has a barb on the end for skewering grubs. Yummy!

Austrians were puzzled when they found a dead shark on a freshwater riverbank. A chef eventually confessed – he had put it there as a joke when it began to smell as he defrosted it for a buffet!

An elephant produces around 150 kg (330 lb) of dung every day.

Birds can eat berries that are highly poisonous to humans.

The total combined weight of the world's ant population is heavier than the combined weight of the human population.

Chalkbrood is a fungal disease that destroys honeybee larvae and gives them a chalky white appearance.

Both male and female octopuses die shortly after mating.

Dachshund means "badger dog": the dogs were originally bred for killing badgers, rabbits, and foxes. Not so cute, then!

Bat bugs look like bed bugs and suck the blood of bats.

A giant catfish frightened divers in a Dutch holiday park. The monster fish was found to be 2.3 m (7 ft 6 in) long and ate three ducks a day, but staff promised that it wouldn't eat people!

Sea pigs are a type of sea cucumber: they live in really deep oceans, rolling around in the mud on the seabed and eating it!

The postman caterpillar eats poisonous leaves. It feeds on cyanide-filled passionflower leaves and stores the poison in its spikes to put off predators.

Big, fat atlas beetle larvae can bite when touched.

One pat of elephant dung can contain up to 7,000 dung beetles!

Incredibly Strange Animal Quiz

ANiMAL QUiZ 1

1 What is the yucky green algae found covering many ponds called?

a) pond slime
b) pond goo
c) pond muck

2 How many teaspoons of blood can a gruesome vampire bat suck from its victim in one go?

a) 5
b) 15
c) 55

3 Where do the worm-like larvae of the human botfly like to live?

a) on your eyelashes
b) under your skin
c) up your bottom

1 SLIME BONUS POINT

4 Why is the assassin bug sometimes called the "kissing bug"?

a) its lips are kiss-shaped
b) it kisses its mate, then kills it
c) it bites human lips to drink blood

REALLY HORRID!

5 How do some types of leaf beetle protect their eggs?

a) they wrap them in poop
b) they bury them in spit
c) they hide them in vomit

6 By what gruesome method does a boa constrictor kill its victims?

a) it chews them to death
b) it squeezes them to death
c) it injects them with poison

7 What happens to a starfish if you chop off one of its arms?

a) the arm keeps on wiggling
b) it swims in circles
c) it grows a new arm

8 How big is the pulsing heart of a blue whale, the world's largest animal?

a) the size of a pea
b) the size of a car
c) the size of a football

1 SLIME BONUS POINT

9 What can a maggot-infested body reveal to the police?

a) how long the body has been dead
b) what the person ate for dinner
c) who committed the crime

10 On which animal's tongue does the gross tongue-eating louse live?

a) a fish
b) a crocodile
c) a turtle

Answers on page 298

ANiMAL QUiZ 2

1 How can the poison from the bite of a carpet viper kill you?

a) it makes you bleed inside
b) it eats away at your brain
c) it paralyzes your throat

2 What drink is made from beans found in the poop of the tree-climbing civet cat?

a) tea
b) coffee
c) hot chocolate

3 How many mice would a cat have to eat to get the same amount of nutrition as in a tin of cat food?

a) 50
b) 15
c) 5

1 SLIME BONUS POINT

4 Which thumb-sized animal has such vicious teeth that it can pierce the tough skin of a cow?

a) a killer bee
b) a vampire bat
c) a soldier ant

5 Where does the slimy Surinam toad lay her eggs?

a) in the skin on her back
b) under her tongue
c) between her toes

1 SLIME BONUS POINT

6 **What is really creepy about a moray eel?**

a) it has two sets of teeth
b) its eye sockets are empty
c) its mouth is glued together

8 **What does a wild jackal most like to sink its teeth into?**

a) decomposing fruit
b) rotting meat
c) live mealworms

7 **If you let a safari ant bite a wound, then break off its body, what happens?**

a) its jaws act like stitches
b) its mouth numbs the pain
c) its tongue cleans the blood

TOO STINKY!

9 **What gross thing does the giant lizard, the Komodo dragon, occasionally eat?**

a) its own poop
b) its toenails
c) human corpses

10 **What did a seal once do to a woman when she tried to rescue it?**

a) it kissed her on the lips
b) it bit her nose off
c) it farted in her face

Answers on page 298

1 Where in the world can you drink a smoothie made from liquidized frogs?

a) Peru
b) France
c) China

2 How does the hideous eel-like lamprey devour its fishy prey?

a) it crunches it up
b) it swallows it whole
c) it sucks it dry

3 The odorous house ant lives in the USA. If you squash it, what does it smell of?

a) rotten coconuts
b) old boiled eggs
c) rancid fat

1 SLIME BONUS POINT

4 Which of these deadly snakes might spit in your eyes?

a) a cobra
b) a viper
c) a taipan

5 What crazy thing can happen when two Montana mountain goats butt heads too hard?

a) their heads explode
b) their hooves fall off
c) their horns bend

6 How long are the razor-sharp teeth of a gruesome viperfish?

a) half the length of its head
b) the same length as its head
c) twice the length of its head

7 What can the cassowary bird do with the hideous spiked claw on its foot?

a) spear a fish
b) clean its teeth
c) kill a human

8 Stumpy the duck was born with what unusual feature?

a) two heads
b) four legs
c) three ears

9 How does a killer whale attack a shark?

a) it wrenches its head off
b) it rips its fins off
c) it rams its stomach

10 Why do giant Komodo dragon lizards vomit up their food before a fight?

a) to scare their opponent
b) so they can move faster
c) to snack on later

1 SLIME BONUS POINT

Answers on page 298

AniMAL QUIZ 4

1 Which fish eats a poisonous meal before it dies so creatures feeding on it will die too?

    a) a swordfish

    b) a marlin

    c) a barracuda

2 Which octopus has a deadly venom in its saliva that can kill a human?

    a) a blue-ringed octopus

    b) a giant octopus

    c) a reef octopus

3 What is another name for a hagfish?

    a) a slime eel

    b) a dogfish

    c) a stinkhorn

1 SLIME BONUS POINT

4 What vile thing does the "butcher bird" do to its prey before eating it?

    a) sticks it on a spike

    b) smashes its skull

    c) breaks off its legs

5 What happens to your skin when you get stung by a tropical fire ant?

    a) it catches fire

    b) it fills with pus

    c) it turns black

6 What does the Garra rufa fish like to nibble?

a) dead skin on people's feet
b) human nail clippings
c) human corpses

7 What was bat poop used for in the American Civil War?

a) to make gunpowder
b) to camouflage soldiers' faces
c) to snack on for energy

8 Which buzzing bug feasts only on the rotting flesh of dead bodies?

a) a fruit fly
b) a flesh fly
c) a flesh butterfly

1 SLIME BONUS POINT

9 What does a female scorpion do after mating?

a) vomit on her mate
b) eat her mate
c) kiss her mate

10 In which animal's stomach have people found horses' heads and bicycle parts?

a) a cow's
b) a hippo's
c) a shark's

Answers on page 298

ANiMAL QUiZ 5

1 **What is a cockroach's skin covered with?**

a) a green slime
b) an oily coating
c) a gooey gel

2 **How many pulsating hearts does an octopus have?**

a) one
b) two
c) three

3 **Baby jewel wasps hatch inside a cockroach's stomach. How do they get out?**

a) they crawl out through its bottom
b) they eat their way out
c) they fly out of its ears

REALLY HORRID!

4 **What is 3 percent of the ice in Antarctica made up of?**

a) penguin pee
b) albatross poop
c) seal fat

1 SLIME BONUS POINT

5 **Which deceptively cute bird has a barbed tongue to skewer grubs?**

a) a robin
b) a hummingbird
c) a woodpecker

6 Why does an eel spin large prey in its mouth and break it up before eating it?

a) to get the blood out
b) to make it bite-sized
c) to get the guts out

7 What is the only way to break the grip of the Gila monster lizard when it bites you?

a) drown it
b) tickle it
c) scream at it

8 Which of these animals feeds its babies by vomiting up food?

a) an octopus
b) a bird
c) a lizard

9 How many bone-crunching teeth does the average crocodile have in its jaws?

a) 20–30
b) 60–80
c) 150–200

10 Why does a bombardier beetle shoot out a stinky liquid from its bottom?

a) to feed its babies
b) to clean it out
c) to scare its enemies

1 SLIME BONUS POINT

Answers on page 298

ANiMAL QUiZ 6

1 What is it called when a crocodile twists its body and bites down hard to rip off a piece of its prey?

a) a death roll
b) a kill spin
c) a somersault

2 Which creepy creature can survive by eating glue from a postage stamp?

a) a cockroach
b) an earwig
c) a beetle

3 Where is one of the few places a naked mole rat has hair?

a) inside its ears
b) inside its behind
c) inside its mouth

REALLY HORRID!

4 Which beetle uses animal fur coated with its fluid from its own backside to make a nest?

a) a scarab beetle
b) a burying beetle
c) a blister beetle

1 SLIME BONUS POINT

5 Why does a hagfish tie itself in a knot and then sneeze?

a) to get snot out of its body
b) to help it poop properly
c) to cure a cold

6 Why do leatherback turtles have sharp spines in their throats?

a) to stop prey from escaping
b) to pick their teeth clean
c) to spear fish

7 How do weaver ants spin the silk for their nests?

a) they use earwax
b) they squeeze it out of their babies
c) they stitch flies' legs together

8 What is the name for the type of lice that infest your underwear?

a) worm lice
b) beetle lice
c) crab lice

1 SLIME BONUS POINT

9 What would happen to a rat's teeth if it stopped gnawing at hard materials?

a) they would curl
b) they would fall out
c) they would grow into its brain

10 Which gruesome sea creature can bend its jaws back to an angle of 180 degrees?

a) a tubeworm
b) a gulper eel
c) a giant squid

1 SLIME BONUS POINT

Answers on page 298

ANIMAL QUIZ ANSWERS

Animal Quiz 1

1) a   2) a   3) b   4) c   5) a   6) b   7) c   8) b   9) a   10) a

Animal Quiz 2

1) a   2) b   3) c   4) b   5) a   6) a   7) a   8) b   9) c   10) b

Animal Quiz 3

1) a   2) c   3) a   4) a   5) b   6) a   7) a   8) b   9) c   10) a

Animal Quiz 4

1) c   2) a   3) a   4) a   5) b   6) b   7) a   8) b   9) b   10) c

Animal Quiz 5

1) b   2) c   3) b   4) a   5) c
6) b   7) a   8) b   9) b   10) c

Animal Quiz 6

1) a   2) a   3) c   4) a   5) a
6) a   7) b   8) c   9) a   10) b

Incredibly Strange Random Facts

The Empire State Building is struck by lightning about 100 times every year.

By the time the average American child is 18, they will have seen around 16,000 violent acts and 8,000 murders on television.

The Roman emperor Caligula had the tomb of Alexander the Great opened up so that he could wear his protective breatsplate! Now that's a really horrible hand-me-down!

The Eiffel Tower in Paris gets up to 15 cm (6 in) taller in summer, when the weather is hot and its iron frame expands.

Fake snow used to be made from asbestos, so people would have sprinkled the toxic mineral around their homes!

Queen Cleopatra of Egypt married two of her own brothers!

During the 1990's famine in North Korea, starving people dug up and ate human bodies.

Eric Livingstone ate 1.3 kg (3 lb) of haggis in eight minutes in 2008.

Some parasitic worms can grow up to 30 cm (1 ft) inside the human body and then leave it through any available hole or gap, including the corner of the eye!

A sick Yorkshire Terrier was found by a vet to have swallowed eight party balloons. After they were removed, it must have felt a little deflated!

Bao Xishun, one of the world's tallest men, saved the lives of two dolphins in 2006 by reaching into their stomachs with his long arms, which measure 1.06 m (42 in), and removing pieces of plastic.

Dropping something on the floor for even five seconds can contaminate it with bacteria.

A Victorian doctor invented a trap for tapeworms (parasitic worms that live in the human gut). It was a little metal cage, baited with something tasty for the tapeworms. The patient had to swallow it on a string and wait for the tapeworm to spring the trap, when it would be pulled out of the body. Some people choked to death in the process!

In the UK, a cat stuck on a viaduct 27 m (90 ft) high had to be rescued by the firefighters using a hydraulic platform.

A dog's sense of smell is tens of thousands of times better than a human's.

Fifteen people in the USA die every year from dog attacks.

Red rain fell in the Indian state of Kerala in 2001. The reason is still a mystery, but theories range from algae spores or pollution, to the blood of bats or extraterrestrials!

The Japanese believe that a clean toilet brings good fortune. They even have books on the subject!

A cheese containing live maggots is a traditional delicacy in Italy. The Casu Marzu is brought out on special occasions despite the fact that it can make you very ill!

The American state of Florida is bigger than the whole of England.

Australia has a plague of poisonous cane toads, which can grow to be the size of a small dog. The government asked people to kill them humanely, but most Australians just bash them over the head!

A Japanese man was so angry at a new building blocking out his light that he shot it, causing lots of damage and getting himself arrested!

Girls who made matches in the 1800's often suffered from "phossy jaw" – their jaw bones would rot away, poisoned by the phosphorus used to make the matches.

In an attempt to waterproof their boots, soldiers in the First World War would use a grease made from whale oil. Bet their feet smelt lovely!

It is said that the Romans used to dye their hair with a fermented mixture of leeches and vinegar.

The biggest ever swarm of locusts contained 10 billion of the creatures!

According to legend, when pharaoh Amenhotep (1427–1400BC) defeated a rebellion in Nubia, southern Egypt, he killed 312 people in a single hour and took home the right hands of all his victims.

In some places in America, you can get brain sandwiches made from deep-fried calves brains! Pass the bucket!

A scatologist is someone who devotes their life to studying poop in all its forms.

Sometimes a pig's heart valve can be used to replace a human's faulty one.

Did you know that in some places, chocolate chip cookies are baked using flour from dried and ground up mealworms?

A medieval punishment for murderers was to have each arm and leg tied to a different horse, then the four horses were made to run in different directions, tearing the criminal apart.

A Nebraska man saved his dog with the kiss of life after it fell into an icy lake while chasing geese.

In Hong Kong you can buy packets of deep-fried crab.

A Korean delicacy called *sannaki* is made of baby octopuses which are still live and wriggling! Ew!

The fourth funnel on the *Titanic* was just for show. The designers thought four would look more impressive than three.

You have roughly 2 million stinky sweat glands on your body.

Tattooing criminals with symbols that marked them out as outcasts was a common punishment in medieval Japan. In one region, all criminals had the symbol for a dog tattooed on their foreheads.

Kangaroos cause over 20,000 road crashes a year in Australia.

In the early 1920s, the Italian fascists would intimidate their socialist enemies by feeding them large amounts of castor oil (a laxative) then tying them to a post so that they couldn't move away.

The first use of toilet paper recorded was in China in the 6th century AD.

It is illegal to keep a gerbil as a pet in California, since gerbils have been known to carry tuberculosis.

In 1973 a Swedish man was buried in a coffin made out of mature cheese.

RANDOM FACTS

Japan has the highest number of vending machines: one for every 23 people. They sell anything from live lobsters to potted plants!

Ancient Romans used to feast on flamingo tongues.

College lecturer Paul Rogerson creates award-winning sculptures … from lard! His subjects range from from Bugs Bunny to Don Quijote, but the sculptures last only two months before they go off and become a bit stinky.

Pilots sometimes dump the contents of a plane's onboard toilet when over the sea.

Your nails grow more quickly as you get older.

The longest time between twins being born was 87 days.

It was customary amongst the ancient Scythian soldiers to drink the urine of the first enemy they killed.

The skeleton of philosopher Jeremy Bentham and wax model of his head attend some meetings at a London university. He is listed as "present but not voting!"

The Japanese delicacy called *shiokara* contains fermented fish guts. Sounds delicious!

Saw-scaled vipers make a sizzling sound.

Rich ancient Roman Vedius Pollio used to feed dead slaves to his pet fish.

People living in the Amazon rainforest like egg dishes ... made with tarantula eggs!

A giant rat in Sweden measuring 38 cm (15 in) munched its way through a concrete wall and into a family's kitchen.

Fried termites are a common snack in North Africa.

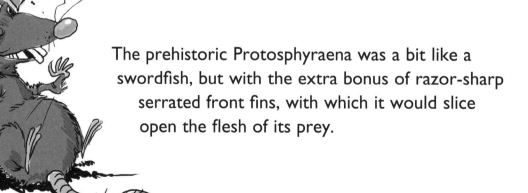

The prehistoric Protosphyraena was a bit like a swordfish, but with the extra bonus of razor-sharp serrated front fins, with which it would slice open the flesh of its prey.

Armadillos have about 100 razor sharp teeth.

The submarine HL *Hunley* was "sunk" three times in its career.

The Celts would stick the heads of their defeated enemies on poles for all to see.

A powder monkey was no ape, but a boy whose job it was to keep the gun crews supplied with gunpowder on old warships.

Lizardfish have a very strange facial arrangement. Their eyes are on their tongues!

In China people bury eggs underground and eat them once they have turned rotten.

The largest leech discovered measured 45 cm (18 in) in length.

Some sneezes shoot out of your body at the speed of a hurricane!

Some old ships were used as floating prisons in the 18th and 19th centuries.

Buddhist monks refused to kill any of the ants infesting their Kuala Lumpur temple because of their beliefs in non-violence ... even when one monk was hospitalized by ant bites!

In Mexico some people eat tacos filled with ants' eggs!

Forest fires move faster when going uphill than downhill.

The paint pigment called Indian Yellow was originally made from the dried urine of cows that had been fed on only mango leaves.

Bulgarian-American singer Bantcho Bantchevsky is most famous for killing himself during the interval of an opera by jumping off a balcony at the Metropolitan Opera House in New York.

Tripe, a nasty-looking dish made from a cow's stomach, is served in different forms all over the world.

A Viking grave found in England in 2009 contained the remains of 51 people, their bodies neatly gathered in one pile of bones and their skulls in another.

Carrion beetles cover snails with digestive juices and suck them out of their shells.

When Leontius of Byzantium deposed Justinian II and took power in AD695, he slit open the previous emperor's nose and tongue.

A Chinese man placed an advert asking for someone to share his grave so he wouldn't be lonely when he died!

No two soldiers of the Chinese terracotta army of 8,000 or so men are exactly alike.

The death cap mushroom is not to be underestimated. It has killed more people than any other poisonous mushroom in Europe.

A giant centipede that lives in the Amazon rainforest of South America has claws that secrete a toxic venom.

Thresher sharks stun their prey by whacking them with their tails before going in for the kill.

The average person spends 3 months of their life on the toilet.

The urine of the cape water buffalo from Africa is so flammable that it can be used as lantern fuel!

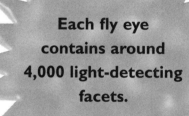

Each fly eye contains around 4,000 light-detecting facets.

Scientists in Japan have isolated a scent in cow dung which is now being used in cosmetics. Who wants a cow dung lipstick?

The box jellyfish is the most venomous type, with a sting that can kill in 4 minutes.

The deepest shipwreck ever found is the *Rio Grande* at 5.7 km (3.5 miles).

Goong Ten means "dancing shrimp" and is a Thai salad dish of live little shrimp.

The deadly stargazer fish can either kill you with its poisonous spines or by giving you an electric shock.

A local delicacy in Cuba is roasted water cockroaches. Mmm, crunchy.

Human urine was regularly used as a mouthwash in Europe until the 1800s.

Botulism is a nasty and sometimes fatal type of food poisoning, which can generally be prevented by proper food preparation.

Gangrene is a horrible infection that makes your body tissue decay and turn black.

The longest cuddle ever lasted for 5,000 years! Archeologists discovered a pair of entwined skeletons in Northern Italy and believe the couple to be from the Neolithic period.

Mosquitoes are more likely to attack you if you eat bananas.

Food poisoning from E.coli bacteria found in undercooked food can range from fairly mild to extremely serious. In some cases, it can turn the human liver to mush!

The Yellowstone National Park in the USA contains a super-volcano that could make most of the country uninhabitable!

Mice are said to like eating cheese, but professional rodent exterminators have found they like peanut butter and bacon just as much.

Carnivorous plants usually slurp up insects but they have been know to eat rats as well!

Some Russian farmers are now producing milk from moose.

A condition called hypertrichosis causes thick hair to grow on people's faces.

Thomas Edison, the inventor of the lightbulb, was said to be afraid of the dark.

There are no clocks in the casinos of Las Vegas so that gamblers not wearing a watch are more likely to spend longer there.

Female pharoah Hatshepsut was often depicted with a false beard.

A kangaroo can disembowel a dog with its powerful hind legs.

In 1924 the state of Nevada introduced the gas chamber as a form of execution.

In 11th-century England, the punishment for a jury member lying in court was to have their hand plunged into boiling water.

One in five people can't remember when they last changed their toothbrush for a nice clean new one!

The longest word in the English language is the name of a lung disease called *pneumonoultramicroscopicsilicovolcano-coniosis*.

Your heart beats around 100,000 times every day.

Burying beetles like to bury their prey, such as mice, to nibble as a tasty snack later.

American Richard Presley lived in an underwater module for 69 days and 19 minutes as part of research into the effects of living under the sea.

The longest species of moray eel – the slender giant moray – can grow up to 4 m (13 ft) in length.

Daredevil Stephen Brown rode a motorcycle through a tunnel of fire that was 51 m (167 ft) long.

A child 1.2 m (4 ft) tall could almost stand upright inside the open mouth of a hippo.

Cola is more acidic than vinegar and acid destroys the enamel on your teeth, so remember to brush properly!

Russian revolutionary Lenin's embalmed body can be visited in a mausoleum in Moscow's Red Square. He died in 1924.

British painter and decorator Nick Male became inundated with jobs when he offered a new service: working naked!

Someone with a bad roundworm infection will vomit worms.

A major zit invasion can turn into cystic acne, where the spots grow larger and become swollen, painful, and pus-filled.

Ancient Egyptians usually slept on pillows made of stone!

Around 78 million North Americans are classed as obese.

When you lick a stamp you are consuming around a tenth of a calorie.

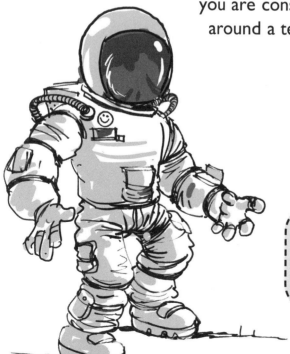

An astronaut returning from space can be up to 5cm (2 in) taller, as the spine expands in microgravity.

If you took out your intestines and uncoiled them, they would be about four times as tall as you.

Henry I of England died in 1135 after eating too many lampreys (a vicious fish like an eel), and being treated by a doctor who gave him medicine to make him go to the toilet.

Around 250 people have fallen off the Leaning Tower of Pisa since it was built.

It only takes about 10 days to die from a total lack of sleep.

Half of the bulk of poop is made up of bacteria.

The shark's sense of smell is greater than any other fish – it can detect one part of blood in 100 million parts of water.

RANDOM FACTS

An Indonesian pig called the *babirusa* has long curved horns that grow up from its nose. In old animals, the horns sometimes grow in a complete circle and pierce the jaw. A bit of a design flaw!

Flea eggs don't hatch unless there is a living host, like a dog or cat, nearby to feast on.

Some infections can produce blue pus! This freaky-looking stuff comes from *pseudomonas* bacteria.

Spiders Arabella and Anita were the first of their kind to spin webs in space in 1973!

Astronauts' footprints on the moon will be there for thousands of years as there is no wind to blow them away.

Avalanches kill over 150 people worldwide every year. They are mostly skiers and snowboarders.

Fishermen in the Fens (a wetland area in eastern England) in the 11th century discovered the skeletons of Norman knights, still in their chain-mail, 50 years after they had battled with the Saxons.

The main source of food for animals that live in the deep sea is marine snow flakes of dead things and poop from creatures who live higher up in the water!

Gas that you take in when you eat food takes between 30 and 45 minutes to be released as a fart.

The worst air-show disaster happened in 2002, when a fighter jet crashed into spectators in Ukraine and killed 78 people, injuring more than 100.

French king Louis XIV requested that his heart be embalmed after his death, so when he died in 1715 his heart was mummified. It was stolen during the French Revolution and is said to have been eaten by English geologist William Buckland in the 19th century!

The Australian bloodwood tree oozes red sap that looks like blood when it is cut.

The oldest known living tree is the Great Basin bristlecone pine in California, at well over 5,000 years old.

The nail fungus onychomycosis can turn your nails green.

It takes
20 minutes for a
leech to fill itself
up with human
blood.

During the first games at the Colosseum in Rome in AD80, over 5,000 animals were killed including elephants, tigers, lions, elks, hyenas, hippopotamuses, and giraffes.

If a cockroach loses a leg, it can grow another!

In Japan you can munch on dried fish snacks instead of peanuts and crackers with your cola or soda.

A bad gum infection called gingivitis can lead to pus-filled mouth sores, purple gums, and the stinkiest of stinky breath.

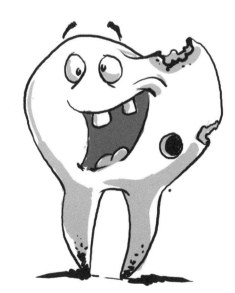

RANDOM FACTS

Being cold in the night tends to give you bad dreams. The colder the room, the more likely you are to have a bad dream. Wrap up warm tonight!

The Persian king, Xerxes, wanted to take a large army over a stretch of water called the Hellespont so he built a bridge. When a storm destroyed the bridge, Xerxes was so angry, he punished the river by having a soldier whip it!

Cat urine glows in the dark under ultraviolet light.

Two American scientists have made a computer mouse that is fitted inside the skin of a real, dead mouse. Gross!

An earthworm tastes with its whole body – it has taste receptors spread all over it.

The longest earthquake lasted for ten minutes in the Sumatra-Andaman Islands.

Akbar the Great, who ruled Mughal India between 1556 and 1605, died in 1605 after being poisoned by his own family.

Necrotizing fasciitis or the "flesh-eating bug" causes your flesh to rot, die, and fall off. It can be fatal, and even people who recover often lose whole chunks of their bodies. Yuk.

An American restaurant produced the world's biggest burger for a charity event. It contained a 48-kg (80-lb) beef patty and 160 cheese slices!

Enormous hailstones damaged around 70,000 homes and injured 400 people during a 1984 storm in Munich, making it the worst damage toll from a hailstorm.

A type of amoeba (single-celled organism) that lives in warm rivers, lakes, and even some swimming pools can infect people if the water gets up their nose. It eats their brain away and they die within two weeks. Although rare, death-by-amoeba is becoming more common! Scary!

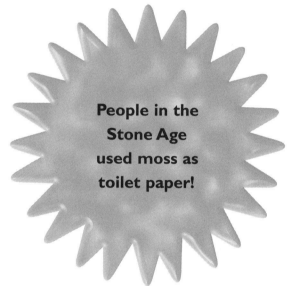

People in the Stone Age used moss as toilet paper!

The matamata turtle moves so slowly that algae grow on its shell. But when it eats, it sucks in large fish with a gulp so fast that it can't be seen with the naked eye!

In ancient times, when a man became a gladiator, he had to sign a contract agreeing to let his employers burn him, chain him up, whip him, and even kill him. Not great terms of employment!

The bad smell of poop comes from chemicals produced by bacteria that break down the food in your gut.

The Black Death lasted three years, killing 25 million people – a third of the European population.

A body left unburied in a tropical climate will be reduced to a skeleton in two weeks by the action of insects.

The lasting pain from an Arizona bark scorpion's sting feels like a series of electric shocks.

Before they are born, developing human babies have a tail, and some developing snake babies have legs. Perhaps we have more in common with snakes than we think!

The tough little tadpoles of some species of frog are able to live inside a pitcher plant without being dissolved by its acidic juices.

A cup of gladiator's blood was given as a cure for epilepsy in ancient Rome.

Most human mutations happen on the Y chromosome, which only occur in men.

Falling coconuts kill ten times more people than sharks do every year.

The fastest lava flow burst from the volcano Nyiragongo in the Democratic Republic of Congo at 60 km (40 miles) per hour.

From the 13th century onward, the samurai began to dominate Japan. A samurai's two-handed sword, the *katana*, could slice a man in half with a single stroke.

Ivan the Terrible beat his own son to death in a fit of rage.

A Tudor cure for asthma consisted of the lungs of a fox mixed with wine and liquorice.

Baby body lice suck blood five times a day.

The highest temperature recorded in the shade was 58 degrees Celsius (136 degrees Fahrenheit) at Al 'Aziziyah in Libya. That was in 1922, before anyone had even heard of global warming!

It takes 20 minutes for a leech to fill itself up with human blood.

Life expectancy in Tudor England was just 35 years, less than half of the average life expectancy in England today.

King Alexandros I of Greece died in 1920 from blood poisoning, after being bitten by his pet monkey.

A woman in England built an extension to her historic house using plaster and human hair!

The law in the USA allows 30 insect fragments to be present in every 100 g (1 oz) of peanut butter. On average, there is also one rodent hair too. Ew!

Incredibly Strange Random Quiz

RANDOM QUIZ 1

1 In ancient times, what did the Scythian soldiers from Central Asia drink after they had killed their first enemy?

a) his blood
b) his urine
c) his spit

2 How many leaf-munching locusts were there in the biggest swarm ever?

a) 10 million
b) 10 billion
c) 10 trillion

3 What happens to the Eiffel Tower in summer?

a) it gets taller
b) it gets shorter
c) it gets fatter

4 What animal's heart valve is sometimes used as a replacement in human hearts?

a) pig
b) sheep
c) duck

1 SLIME BONUS POINT

5 Up to how many squidgy eggs can a slime-oozing slug lay in one go?

a) 10
b) 100
c) 1,000

6 In China, which animal's paws are roasted in clay to help remove the fur before eating them?

a) cat
b) dog
c) bear

7 Why did the Romans collect urine from public toilets?

a) to use it as a clothes dye
b) to drink it
c) to wash in it

1 SLIME BONUS POINT

8 What happened to the Greek messenger, Pheidippides, when he finished running the first marathon in 490BC?

a) he fell into a pile of horse manure
b) he was trampled by a herd of cows
c) he died of exhaustion

TOO STINKY!

9 Each year in Australia there are over 20,000 road crashes caused by which animal?

a) ostrich
b) koala bear
c) kangaroo

10 What does the Peruvian booby bird make from its own droppings?

a) a nest
b) a sculpture
c) its dinner

Answers on page 352

RANDOM QUIZ 2

1 Your delicate squidgy brain sits inside your skull. What is it surrounded by?

a) spinal fluid
b) thick blood
c) jelly

2 What happened to American William Bullock, inventor of the rotary printing press?

a) he was killed by his own invention
b) his invention drove him insane
c) his invention put him in prison

3 Which animals slurp up the snot in fish gills for a slimy snack?

a) sea fleas
b) sea lice
c) sea flies

1 SLIME BONUS POINT

4 Where are eggs buried underground and eaten once they have turned rotten?

a) China
b) Canada
c) Colombia

5 In 1973 a Swedish man was buried in a coffin made of what?

a) chocolate
b) dried poop
c) stinky cheese

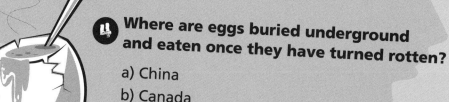

6 Which straggly body hair grows quickest on a man?

a) his nose hair
b) his armpit hair
c) his beard

7 Roughly how many times does your pulsating heart beat in a year?

a) 35 thousand
b) 35 million
c) 35 trillion

8 In which unusual place do lizardfish have their teeth?

a) on their eyes
b) in their nose
c) on their tongue

9 Pickled tripe is served in New England, USA. What is it made from?

a) a cow's stomach
b) a sheep's brain
c) a pig's trotter

10 What did the gruesome ancient Celts do with the heads of people they killed in battle?

a) put them in a stew
b) stick them on a pole
c) use them to play soccer

1 SLIME BONUS POINT

Answers on page 352

RANDOM QUIZ 3

1 Where was it the custom for a woman to mash an "ugly looking" potato into the face of the next man she saw?
a) ancient Greece
b) ancient Rome
c) ancient Peru

2 What was female pharoah Hatshepsut sometimes depicted wearing?
a) pants
b) a beard
c) a hat

3 How many eggs can a blood-sucking head louse lay on your head in its short 30-day life?

a) 10 to 20
b) 100 to 200
c) 1,000 to 2,000

4 What weird taste of porridge does one English restaurant have on its menu?

a) chili
b) fish
c) snail

1 SLIME BONUS POINT

5 What does a vampire bat do while sucking blood from a victim?

a) it pees
b) it poops
c) it sings

6 What can shoot out of your body at the same speed as a hurricane?

a) a smelly fart
b) a loud sneeze
c) projectile vomit

1 SLIME BONUS POINT

7 What did the ancient Assyrians do after skinning their enemies?

a) make slippers from the skins
b) hang the skins on the city wall
c) make rugs from the skins

8 Which scaly critter has teeth that are almost transparent?

a) an iguana
b) a crocodile
c) a tortoise

9 Why were small children pushed up narrow chimneys in the 19th century?

a) to look for Santa
b) to clean out the dirt
c) to keep them quiet

10 If you lined up all your lost eyelashes over a lifetime, roughly how far would they stretch?

a) the length of one bus
b) the length of three buses
c) the length of ten buses

Answers on page 352

RANDOM QUIZ 4

1 If you left two flies alone to mate for a year, how many babies would they make?

a) enough to fill a swimming pool
b) enough to fill a country
c) enough to fill planet Earth

1
SLIME
BONUS
POINT

2 How many wives of English King Henry VIII had their heads chopped off?

a) one
b) two
c) three

3 In Cambodia, what is sometimes added to rice wine to make it taste better?

a) spiders
b) maggots
c) fish eggs

4 Which animal kills its prey by firing a poisonous harpoon from its mouth?

a) a cone snail
b) a killer crab
c) a shooter snail

REALLY HORRID!

5 What are the ghost moth larvae that Aboriginal Australians eat raw known as?

a) witches' grubs
b) witchetty grubs
c) grisly grubs

6 Roughly how many smelly sweat glands do you have on your body?

a) 2,000
b) 2 million
c) 200 million

7 What did Leontius of Byzantium do to the previous emperor when he took power in AD695?

a) slit his nose and tongue
b) slit his ear and cheek
c) plucked out his eyeballs

8 In the 1920s, certain scenes were cut from Hollywood movies shown in Japan. What couldn't they watch?

a) mud wrestling
b) kissing
c) feet scrubbing

9 What was Thomas Edison, inventor of the lightbulb, scared of?

a) mice
b) bats
c) the dark

10 Why do leeches still suck your blood even if you cut them in half?

a) they feel nothing while feeding
b) their jaws get stuck
c) they love blood too much

1 SLIME BONUS POINT

Answers on page 352

RANDOM QUIZ 5

1 How far can a stinkbug spit foul-smelling goo to defend itself from attack?

a) 10 cm (4 in)
b) 20 cm (8 in)
c) 30 cm (1 ft)

2 Which animal's tongue was scoffed at some ancient Roman feasts?

a) whale
b) dog
c) flamingo

1 SLIME BONUS POINT

3 Where are green ants nibbled by children as a snack?

a) West Africa
b) North Australia
c) South America

4 What can make the temperature of your farts hotter than normal?

a) exercise
b) a spicy curry
c) a fever

5 Where do more than 700 kinds of bacteria lurk inside your body?

a) in your intestines
b) in your liver
c) in your brain

6 Which of these things is a newborn baby born with?

a) a third eyelid
b) soft kneecaps
c) an egg tooth

7 What did Vedius Pollio, a rich ancient Roman, regularly feed to his pet fish?

a) his toenail clippings
b) minced dog
c) dead slaves

1 SLIME BONUS POINT

8 Which male critter has a poisonous spur on its hind foot?

a) a spike-footed duck
b) a duck-billed platypus
c) a spiny-tailed mole

9 What creature did the United States army plan to use to drop bombs on Japan in the Second World War?

a) a flying squirrel
b) a turkey vulture
c) a free-tailed bat

10 How long does the average person spend on the toilet in their lives?

a) 3 weeks
b) 3 months
c) 3 years

Answers on page 352

RANDOM QUIZ 6

1 What do Native Alaskans bury in a jar and eat when rotten?

a) salmon eggs
b) sheep heads
c) bear paws

2 How did fearless Celtic queen Boudicca kill herself in AD60?

a) she poisoned herself
b) she drowned herself
c) she sliced off her own head

3 What part of the human body does a blood-sucking mosquito like to feed on most?

a) hairy armpits
b) sweaty feet
c) snotty noses

1 SLIME BONUS POINT

4 Which beetle covers a snail with digestive juices and sucks it out of its shell to eat it?

a) a carrion beetle
b) a French beetle
c) a slurper beetle

5 What eggs are used to make a bizarre egg dish in the Amazon?

a) parrot
b) turtle
c) tarantula

6 Which animal started a short but deadly war between Greece and Bulgaria in 1925 when it crossed the border?

a) a mouse
b) a kangaroo
c) a dog

7 The first use of what was recorded in China in the 6th century AD?

a) toilet paper
b) toothpaste
c) razor

8 What causes you to go bright red when you blush?

a) your blood vessels burst
b) blood rushes through your blood vessels
c) your brain tells your skin to turn red

9 How many eyelids does a camel have to protect it from sand and the sun?

a) two
b) three
c) four

10 How many live scorpions has Rene Alvarenga of El Salvador eaten?

a) 35,000
b) 3,500
c) 350

1 SLIME BONUS POINT

Answers on page 352

RANDOM QUIZ ANSWERS

Random Quiz 1

1) a   2) b   3) b   4) a   5) b   6) c   7) a   8) c   9) c   10) a

Random Quiz 2

1) a   2) a   3) b   4) a   5) a   6) c   7) b   8) c   9) a   10) b

Random Quiz 3

1) c   2) b   3) b   4) c   5) a   6) b   7) b   8) a   9) b   10) b

Random Quiz 4

1) c   2) b   3) a   4) a   5) b   6) b   7) a   8) b   9) c   10) a

Random Quiz 5

1) c   2) c   3) b   4) c   5) a
6) b   7) c   8) b   9) c   10) b

Random Quiz 6

1) a   2) a   3) b   4) a   5) c
6) c   7) a   8) b   9) b   10) a